Critical Thinking and Professional Judgement for Social Work

SAGE was founded in 1965 by Sara Miller McCune to support the dissemination of usable knowledge by publishing innovative and high-quality research and teaching content. Today, we publish more than 850 journals, including those of more than 300 learned societies, more than 800 new books per year, and a growing range of library products including archives, data, case studies, reports, and video. SAGE remains majority-owned by our founder, and after Sara's lifetime will become owned by a charitable trust that secures our continued independence.

Los Angeles | London | New Delhi | Singapore | Washington DC

Critical Thinking and Professional Judgement for Social Work

Fourth Edition

LYNNE RUTTER AND KEITH BROWN

Series Editor Keith Brown

Los Angeles | London | New Delhi
Singapore | Washington DC

Learning Matters
An imprint of SAGE Publications Ltd
1 Oliver's Yard
55 City Road
London EC1Y 1SP

SAGE Publications Inc.
2455 Teller Road
Thousand Oaks, California 91320

SAGE Publications India Pvt Ltd
B 1/I 1 Mohan Cooperative Industrial Area
Mathura Road
New Delhi 110 044

SAGE Publications Asia-Pacific Pte Ltd
3 Church Street
#10-04 Samsung Hub
Singapore 049483

Editor: Kate Wharton
Development editor: Lauren Simpson
Production controller: Chris Marke
Project management: Swales & Willis Ltd,
Exeter, Devon
Marketing manager: Camille Richmond
Cover design: Wendy Scott
Typeset by: C&M Digitals (P) Ltd, Chennai, India
Printed in Great Britain by Henry Ling Limited
at The Dorset Press, Dorchester, DT1 1HD

First published in 2006
Second edition published in 2008
Third edition published in 2012 (Previously published
as *Critical Thinking for Social Work.*)
Fourth edition published in 2015

Library of Congress Control Number: 2015940820

British Library Cataloguing in Publication data

A catalogue record for this book is available from the
British Library

ISBN 978-1-4739-1918-1
ISBN 978-1-4739-1919-8 (pbk)

National Centre for Post-Qualifying Social Work and Professional Practice at Bournemouth University

Welcome to one of our publications to support students undertaking post-qualifying learning.

The various books have been specifically designed and written to support students and we hope you find them of value to both your study and practice of social work.

The texts have been written by experienced practitioners and are therefore up to date with issues for social work practice.

Professor Keith Brown
Director of the National Centre for Post-Qualifying Social Work and Professional Practice, Bournemouth University

Contents

viii

Foreword: a series to support post-qualifying social work

This text, *Critical Thinking and Professional Judgement for Social Work*, is one of a series of texts written by experienced social work educators and practitioners, some of whom are working at the National Centre for Post-Qualifying Social Work and Professional Practice at Bournemouth University.

All the texts are written with the specific aim of supporting social workers who are undertaking post-qualifying studies in their chosen field of practice/specialism. However, many social work students and their educators on qualifying programmes have also found the text useful, as have post-registration health professionals working within the integrated health and social care agenda.

As members of the National Centre for Post-Qualifying Social Work and Professional Practice, we all work with the aim of promoting the best health and social work practice for the sake of all service users, patients and their carers.

I trust that you will find this text of real value in your career.

Professor Keith Brown
Director of the National Centre for Post-Qualifying Social Work and Professional Practice

About the authors

Dr Lynne Rutter specialises in professional educational development within post-qualifying (PQ) and continuing professional development (CPD) programmes at the National Centre for Post-Qualifying Social Work and Professional Practice at Bournemouth University. Here she has helped design and develop a number of units for both health and social care markets. She facilitates learning about critical thinking, professional reasoning and judgement, evidencing professional learning, leading and enabling others and service improvement methodology. Lynne's professional and research interests focus on the nature and development of professional reasoning and judgement, and her Professional Doctorate has helped create a unique set of assessment criteria for their development and evaluation within academic written work.

Professor Keith Brown holds professional qualifications in nursing, social work and teaching, and academic qualifications in nursing, social work and management. He has worked in the education and training field for over 30 years, working for three universities and three local authority social work departments. Currently, he is the Director of the National Centre for Post-Qualifying Social Work and Professional Practice at Bournemouth University and the Director of the Centre for Leadership Impact and Management at Bournemouth. In 2005 he was awarded the Linda Ammon Memorial Award, sponsored by the then Department for Education and Skills, a prize awarded to the individual making the greatest contribution to training and education in the UK. His main academic interest lies in the fusion of academia and professional practice to help improve professional thinking and practice.

Preface to the fourth edition

We have been delighted with the responses to the first three editions of this text and especially to hear that a wide range of students and practitioners have found it valuable in their studies and with reflection on their practice. We would like to thank all those who have offered comments and suggestions to us; these have been invaluable in our revision of the content.

This fourth edition has been updated throughout to take account of social work educational reforms and drivers, in particular the ongoing review of the *Professional Capabilities Framework, The College of Social Work (England) 2012*, which was still being developed when the previous edition was published, and its uncertain future with the closure of The College of Social Work, plus the Department of Education's work on social work Knowledge and Skills Statements (KSS). We have also taken account of the many recent health and social care reforms, inquiries and reports (e.g. *The Health and Social Care Act 2012*; *The Francis Report 2013*), with their emphasis on developing and enhancing integrated care, quality and patient-centred cultures. These reforms and proposals obviously impact on professional health and social care education, but perhaps more importantly they continue to prioritise the continuing development of sound critical thinking, professional reasoning and judgement. These topics were the main additions to the third edition and are developed further here. As noted above, our texts are primarily written with the specific aim of supporting social workers who are undertaking post-qualifying studies. However, within an integrated health and social care agenda we understand that much of the content is also relevant to a wide range of health professionals, and we have used it within our own teaching to 'mixed' groups of CPD students. This edition reflects such usage by continuing to take a generic approach to many of the ideas and activities, with the aim of allowing students and ongoing professional learners to think about them in relation to their own situational needs, as they would need to do in practice. For those who require more specific and detailed material, or case studies in relation to professional judgement and decision-making within social work practice, we suggest other titles in this series, e.g. *Professional Decision Making and Risk in Social Work* and *Continuing Professional Development in Social Care.*

We are more than ever aware that there is much to celebrate with respect to health and social work practice as practitioners continue to work skilfully and creatively with all members of society. We sincerely hope this text develops your understanding and ability to think critically in its most holistic sense, enhancing your continuing learning and, therefore, your professional development and expertise.

Dr Lynne Rutter
Professor Keith Brown

Introduction

Critical thinking as a process can appear formal and academic, something far removed from everyday life where decisions have to be taken quickly in less than ideal conditions. It is therefore unhelpful to present critical thinking as a linear process or a set of 'tick-box' techniques for everyday working conditions because we rarely have the time or opportunity to follow a strict order in our thinking. We have adopted a more holistic approach and therefore this work does not aim to be a textbook on critical thinking skills or theories. We do not aim to 'teach' critical thinking. Rather this handbook aims to act as a guide and resource, suggesting ideas from our own practice and the work of others to help you develop your own critical approaches to thinking.

An important review (Phillips and Bond, 2004) found four different conceptions for critical thinking:

- as a generic skill;
- as an embedded skill;
- as a component of lifelong learning;
- for critical being.

All these notions are apparent within the circumstances and requirements of any degree and post-qualifying or post-registration learning. As students and continuing learners you require a set of initial generic and subject-specific critical techniques to work with, but developing critical abilities within a specialist arena will also enhance learning and development and allow you to progress your own style of critical thinking. Our concept of critical thinking encompasses the idea that it should be developed and embedded within existing practice abilities to help a practitioner deal more confidently with an uncertain and ever-changing world.

Our ideas have been developed from practice experience with students over many years, and from our ongoing research and reading on the subject. In order not to interrupt the flow of ideas or detract from the informal style of this guide, we have kept referencing to a minimum.

Structure of the book

The first chapter explores the many different ways this book can help students as well as practitioners with professional development. In the second chapter we look at a useful conception of critical thinking as a set of 'requisite intellectual resources' (Bailin et al., 1999). These generic resources are explored further in the following chapters and are enhanced with more context-specific critical abilities, qualities and approaches appropriate for practice. The book provides chapters on professional judgement, using knowledge in practice, critical reflection, writing, critical practice and lastly continuing learning.

This book takes a pragmatic look at a range of ideas associated with critical thinking and judgement, particularly those linked with professional learning and development. It aims to present a number of ideas which should assist you in understanding and developing your critical thinking knowledge and abilities within your particular area. You are all unique learners and practitioners working in very different professional contexts so we have included a number of questions and activities to help you develop your own ideas and perspectives on this material. If you wish to enhance your understanding in a particular specialist area you will find suggested titles for further reading provided at the end of each chapter.

Chapter 1

Who is this book for and how can it help?

This book is written primarily for post-qualifying and post-registration learners who are developing their practice expertise. However, we would argue that there are a number of ways in which critical thinking, particularly when associated with reflection and experiential learning, becomes an essential part of learning and development on any academic programme, and for many areas of work-based continuing professional development.

How can this book help with learning?

As mentioned in the Introduction, professional health and social care education is continually being influenced by policy and reform, but the continuing development of sound critical thinking, professional reasoning and judgement remains a priority. The ability to think critically can, therefore, be seen to be embedded within a range of formal and informal assessment standards, and within professional requirements.

Academic programmes

Criteria such as working in complex situations, exercising powers and responsibilities, managing risk and making informed decisions are listed as generic final-year undergraduate assessment standards, and are developed further at master's level to include aspects such as creativity, insight and advanced independent thinking (QAAHE, 2008). These qualities involve various cognitive skills and abilities associated with critical thinking – for example, critical analysis, critical reflection, sound reasoning and evaluation. Developing critical thinking abilities and attributes can, therefore, help students extract, express and evaluate the learning and professional development occurring during their studies, placements and/or work-based practice.

Continuing professional development (CPD)

Professionals continue to learn and develop throughout their careers in order to keep their skills and knowledge up to date, and to be able to work safely, legally and effectively. This learning and development can be regulated by, or at least guided by, the use of professional requirements. These professional requirements will usually make reference to the need to improve and enhance levels of thinking within and for practice.

In the social work arena, the Professional Capabilities Framework (PCF) is an over-arching professional standards framework containing nine domains representing the knowledge, skills and values that social workers need to practise effectively and which help to structure and guide their CPD and career activities (The College of Social Work, England, 2012). It sets out consistent expectations of social workers at every stage in their career from initial social work education to continuing professional development well after qualification. Unfortunately, the closure of The College of Social Work has been announced due to increasing financial pressures, and so the future of the PCF is uncertain. For the purposes of this text we will work to the domains and capabilities as established at this point in time, in the hope that another organisation can take over the remit for these professional standards. We therefore recommend you consult the Skills for Care (www.skillsforcare.org.uk) and British Association for Social Work (BASW) websites for revised assessment outcomes. At present, across the nine PCF domains (or areas) there are nine levels of development (see Appendix), from beginning social worker education to a strategic level of practice. Within each level distinct capabilities have been identified that practitioners are expected to evidence with each domain.

It can be seen that many of the domains include elements of critical thinking. For example, Domain 2 (focusing on ethics and values) states that social workers have an *obligation to conduct themselves ethically and to engage in ethical decision-making, including through partnership with people who use their services*. Domain 6 focuses on *applying critical reflection and analysis to inform and provide a rationale for professional decision-making*. This domain identifies the principles of critical thinking and reasoned discernment (augmented by creativity and curiosity) in order to identify, distinguish, evaluate and integrate multiple sources of formal and informal knowledge and evidence. Domain 7 (intervention and skills) focuses on the use of *judgement and authority to intervene with individuals, families and communities to promote independence, provide support and prevent harm, neglect and abuse*.

In addition, progression between levels on the PCF is *characterised by development of people's ability to manage complexity, risk, ambiguity and increasingly autonomous decision making across a range of situations*, and would need to be demonstrated as 'evidence' of professional development for various circumstances. A suggested issue for consideration here is: *the quality of the judgements made, and the level of ability to explain and justify them*. In this respect, critical thinking and professional judgement can be seen to be the underpinning and embedded abilities within and across such 'assessment' processes and structures. We therefore recognise critical thinking as a generic quality, and for this reason have not specifically connected the chapters within this text to any particular domains of the PCF. However, it is important for individuals, and indeed any educators, to ensure that appropriate links are made between the sections of this book, critical thinking development needs and appropriate PCF or other professional standard domains and competences.

Throughout their career, therefore, social work students and practitioners are required to demonstrate integration of all aspects of learning, and provide a sufficiency of evidence across all nine domains, which are seen as being interdependent. For newly qualified social workers, the first step in CPD will be the Assessed and

Supported Year in Employment (ASYE) level. Thereafter, CPD activities will be chosen to enhance an individual's practice of social work in their chosen specialism, or more generally to improve service or staff development, research or leadership skills. The Department of Education has consulted and reported on the range of social work knowledge and skills required for the training, recruitment and retention of social workers at the start of their career. The resulting Knowledge and Skills Statements (KSS) aim to be the basis of the development of national assessment and accreditation systems for adult, and child and family social work professional practice, and include aspects of critical thinking. For example, at the time of going to press one area noted in the KSS for child and family social work (Department of Education, 2014, p17) is: *Analysis, decision making, planning and review,* and incorporates critical thinking elements of *risk and harm assessment, best option setting, testing hypotheses and reaching conclusions, as well as later challenging them if necessary in the light of new evidence.*

Healthcare professional values are mainly driven by the relevant professional bodies, for example, the Nursing and Midwifery Council (NMC) and the British Medical Association (BMA). Health professions have CPD standards and criteria (e.g. the NHS *Knowledge and Skills Framework*) associated with conduct, performance and ethics, where critical thinking abilities and qualities can again be explicitly recognised or more implicitly implied.

All health and social care registrants with the Health and Care Professions Council (HCPC) must undertake CPD to stay registered with them. Their CPD standards state that registrants must maintain a continuous, up-to-date and accurate record of their CPD activities that are a mixture of learning activities relevant to current or future practice, essentially contributing to the quality of their practice and service delivery. In this respect, an understanding of where critical thinking sits within relevant professional requirements should help practitioners identify, evaluate and articulate essential learning and development.

How can this book help with practice?

As practitioners we are expected to take professional responsibility for our own and others' CPD, but employers are also expected to play their part in fostering a culture which values learning and development across the organisation, e.g. providing resources, time and access to learning and research, together with appropriate supervision. The role of leadership in developing and supporting learning cultures is apparent here. A wide range of learning and development activities and opportunities, including in-house training, use of feedback and colleagues, supervision, reflection, case discussion and formal programmes, need to be systematically recorded and recognised as contributing to CPD for the HCPC. The need for reliable assessment of this learning output and impact on practice is also apparent, in order to ensure appropriate evidencing for career progression and professional development or training needs appraisal. Well-led and supportive work-based learning environments play a key role here.

As Rolfe et al. (2011) show, developing practice and learning is difficult to separate. The development of practice is an ongoing activity; it generates experiential knowledge and so to practise is also to learn. The process and outcomes of continuing learning, when meaningfully achieved, will almost naturally embed themselves into processes of working – for example, with more reliable thinking, clearer writing and deeper reflection. Appropriate evaluation of this learning and its impact on practice can ensure that the outputs are fully recognised, recorded and accredited where necessary.

The most important learning, however, is meta-learning – that is, learning about how we learn – and this is the basis of lifelong learning. This handbook, therefore, also focuses on learning as an end in itself and makes critical thinking and practice an integrated way of continuing to develop.

Any profession has always demanded critical abilities and qualities from its practitioners because decisions have to be made 'on the spot' and under pressure. With health and social care practice situations being particular complex arenas, the consequences of any judgements, decisions and action are extremely important, and so the need for critical thinking is ever present. The practitioner is working with uncertainty, risk, diversity and difference in a way that recognises oppression, and works to empower and promote the needs and rights of patients, service users and carers. This requirement goes beyond 'competent practice' and demands 'critical practice' (Adams et al., 2009), and the development of 'critical being', i.e. a person who not only reflects critically on knowledge but also develops their powers of critical self-reflection and critical action (Barnett, 1997).

No matter what we do we cannot escape our thinking but it can often be left unquestioned in our busy lives. We suggest that developing critical thinking can ensure that we use the 'best' thinking we are capable of in any set of circumstances in order to continually refine our professional judgement and expertise.

Chapter 2

Critical thinking: some general principles

Aspects of critical thinking are apparent when you consider, deliberate, analyse, assess, make decisions or judgements, and discuss or debate issues with others, so most practitioners have plenty of skills and experience to build on. We are, therefore, not aiming to teach or present a set of separate techniques but to start you working with some relevant, generic ideas and principles which can develop your own style of critical thinking further.

We do not intend to cover the full range of critical thinking 'skills' (indeed, this would consider them to be something like a checklist, which is inappropriate for practice) but instead highlight a few basic principles to underpin the process of enhancing the critical aspects of your own learning and development.

What's it all about?

Brookfield (1987) shows that critical thinking is a lived and creative activity, not an academic pastime.

> *Being a critical thinker involves more than cognitive activities such as logical reasoning or scrutinising arguments for assertions unsupported by empirical evidence.Thinking critically involves our recognising the assumptions underlying our beliefs and behaviours. It means we can give justifications for our ideas and actions. Most important, perhaps, it means we try to judge the rationality of these justifications. We can do this by comparing them to a range of varying interpretations and perspectives.*
>
> (Brookfield, 1987, pp13–14)

Thinking critically can therefore result in major shifts in our ways of thinking and the development of reflective scepticism, i.e. when nothing is regarded as a universal truth, or taken on trust any more. Our assumptions and beliefs, the views of others and existing structures all start to be questioned, no matter what their basis or authority. It is powerful and transformative stuff and the challenge can be extremely positive. However, critical thinking can also be threatening, provoke anxiety and create adverse reactions from other people. It is hard work, involving self-doubt and mental blocks, but for many it leads to more creative leaps and insights. If you find yourself being adversely affected by the negative aspects, we advise you to seek support.

Critical thinking should not produce cynics but confident people who can be committed to a point of view that is well informed, rational and supported by relevant and valid material for that situation, and who are also open to other ideas.

How can it be achieved?

Because people vary according to their capacities, abilities and experience, how you think critically will be personal to you. To develop this individuality we need an appropriate theory to provide us with valid and useful goals, methods and outcomes, i.e. an underpinning framework and structure. We propose to initially approach the 'how' in our context by using an established theory of Bailin et al. (1999), who suggest that the critical thinker can be thought of in terms of a set of 'requisite intellectual resources'. These ideas have also been used successfully by Ford et al. (2004, 2005) in their research on criticality with students in social work education, and are explored below.

The intellectual resources for critical thinking are:

- background knowledge;
- critical concepts;
- critical thinking standards;
- strategies;
- habits of mind.

We will look at each of these resources in turn and examine their components, why they are thought to be necessary, and where and how they might be of use. We can also identify the ones we need to develop further.

Background knowledge of the situation in question

Bailin et al. (1999, p290) propose that:

> the depth of knowledge, understanding and experience persons have in a particular area of study or practice is a significant determinant of the degree to which they are capable of thinking critically in that area.

In other words, the more you know about a situation and the context in which it sits, the better. This includes existing concepts, beliefs, values and ways of acting, as well as the usual background information which helps clarify the range of available options, e.g. for assessment purposes. However, professional judgement is required to make an informed decision about the actual use of this material. Thus, 'context' plays a significant role in determining what will count as sensible or reasonable application of any standards and principles of critical thinking. This contextually sensitive and moral approach appears well suited to the health and social work arena as it allows for responsible deliberation.

You don't know what you don't know, so can you ensure that you are not missing something important about a practice situation?

How do you find out more – who and what are your sources?

Possession of critical concepts

In order to deliberate responsibly, and appraise all the material or information we are presented with, we need to understand the ideas and language (the concepts) associated with critical thinking. It is too easy to limit thinking about practice to thinking only of practice – that is, we get wrapped up in the detail and specifics of particular cases and the associated decisions and actions, rather than dealing with general underlying issues. For example, an individual practitioner may reflect on a particular judgement by reviewing the available data and decision trail but not realise that he/she was uncritically following the initial but biased 'team view' on the case. Indeed, in many situations general concerns such as the amount of time we have or associated target-driven pressures all reduce our ability to think as carefully and critically as we would like.

Understanding critical thinking allows us to become more aware of these underlying issues and certain natural human tendencies towards bias that we would normally not even recognise. This type of knowledge does run into areas of psychology and human behaviour, but we do not need to study a new discipline here. For much of the time the key is to be able to dig deep enough (usually with the help of others because we can be extremely delusional at times!) and be honest enough to start to recognise the underlying but hidden beliefs, preconceptions and assumptions we have, or we are working with.

There are a number of cognitive and behavioural biases that are pertinent too. Here are a few examples:

- Anchoring effect – tendency to rely too heavily or 'anchor' on one trait or piece of information when making decisions.
- Bandwagon effect – tendency to do or believe things because others do.
- Confirmation bias – tendency to search or interpret information in a way that confirms one's preconceptions.
- Hindsight bias – noted by the Munro Review (Munro, 2011) – distorts our judgement about the predictability of an adverse outcome. When we look backwards it seems clear which assessments or actions were critical in leading to that outcome and we overestimate how visible the signs of danger were.
- Outcome bias – tendency to judge a decision by its eventual outcome rather than the quality of the decision at the time it was made.
- Pseudo-certainty effect – tendency to make risk-averse choices if the expected outcome is positive, but make risk-seeking choices to avoid negative outcomes.

Critical thinking can be largely concerned with distinguishing and understanding various kinds of argument (e.g. Gibbs and Gambrill, 1999; Cottrell, 2013). Although this can be viewed as an academic and mechanistic exercise, it does allow us to realise how easily we form flawed arguments ourselves and accept those that others present to us. We can become more aware of how arguments work and develop the language to critique them properly rather than just 'feeling' there was something wrong with them.

For this part of the book we will focus on formal, logical arguments initially to show key features of the approach. However, it is fully recognised that informal, practical arguments and reasoning are more likely to form the basis of professional judgement in practice, and align with the complexity, uncertainty and contingent nature of work-based decision-making (Kondrat, 1992; Kinsella and Pitman, 2012). For this reason we will critically consider them fully in the following chapter.

Logical arguments

Before we can appraise a formal logical argument we first need to know which type it is, and then have a full understanding regarding its various parts to make appropriate distinctions and evaluate it. Logical arguments are used to suggest the truth or demonstrate the falsity of a particular claim via a formal reasoning process, giving us a viable means for knowing the truth or arriving at sound beliefs. Logical arguments are composed of propositions that are capable of being either true or false, and can serve as the objects of belief – they are the building blocks. The propositions used as reasons/evidence within the argument become the argument's premises. They are the grounds for accepting the argument and its conclusion, which is also the final proposition. There is a movement from one or more propositions used as premises to the proposition argued for as the conclusion.

- This bookcase is wood – proposition/premise.

- Wood is a strong material – proposition/premise.

- This bookcase will support my heavy books – final proposition/conclusion.

The premises must be true and 'accepted', and their relevance to each other and the conclusion must be adequately supported. Premises will differ in their acceptability and credibility, and therefore in their sufficiency to support the conclusion. Any proposition also already carries with it other accepted positions, assumptions or 'givens' that are not always made explicit but which need to be critically examined. In the example above, the words 'strong' and 'heavy' are relative and open to individual interpretation – we will each have a set of established ideas about the types and relative properties of wood that there are.

As the final proposition is arrived at on the basis of one or more other propositions already accepted or known to be true, it is the connection or inference between them which is important in logical argument. The question is whether the truth of the conclusion follows from that of the premises. The problem is that inference, by its nature, is not explicit and needs to be examined. In the example above the key inference would be that the wood the bookshelf is made out of is the right strength for the weight of the books.

Types of logical argument: deductive, inductive and abductive

Deductive arguments

The appropriate logical sequence for a deductive argument moves from the general to the specific, as seen in the above example. A valid argument here is defined as one where the argument's structure actually works as a sequence, even though the propositions (as premises or conclusion) may be false. A sound argument is a valid argument whose premises are all true, so it always arrives at a true conclusion. Be careful not to confuse valid arguments with sound arguments.

Example 1: valid and sound deductive argument. The premises are true, the conclusion is true and the argument's structure is correct.

Premise:	All pilots are people who know how to fly airplanes.
Premise:	John is a pilot.
Conclusion:	John knows how to fly airplanes.

Example 2: valid but unsound deductive argument. One of the premises is false, so the conclusion is false. However, if the premises were all true, then the conclusion would be true because the logical structure works as a sequence and so the argument itself remains a valid one.

Premise:	All tigers are blue.
Premise:	The animal outside my window is a tiger.
Conclusion:	The tiger outside my window is blue.

It is therefore important to note the fact that just because a deductive argument is valid, it does not imply that its conclusion holds true. It is therefore important to always check the accuracy of the premises presented within any argument.

Example 3: invalid deductive argument. The premises are all true but the conclusion actually ends up being false and so the argument is invalid.

Premise:	Fish can swim.
Premise:	My father can swim.
Conclusion:	My father is a fish.

How does this happen? It is usually because of the hidden inferences and assumptions we mentioned above. This refers to anything that is taken for granted, e.g. facts, ideas or beliefs which underlie the argument. For a deductive argument to have a justifiable conclusion (be sound as well as valid) not only must its premises be true, but the inferences which underlie them must also be reasonable and justifiable. As we said, a deductive argument implies from the general to the specific. This is where the problem occurs because other factors in a general statement might be present but not acknowledged. Our example implied that anything that swims must be a fish. We could have worded the proposition as 'only fish can swim' and then it would have been a valid argument at least, although obviously unsound.

Let's look at a more relevant example (from Gibbs and Gambrill, 1999):

Premise: John has an attention-deficit hyperactivity disorder.

Premise: This disorder decreases academic performance.

Premise: Drug X reduces hyperactivity in school children.

Conclusion: If we prescribe drug X for John, his academic performance will improve.

REFLECTION POINT

What are the implications here?

ACTIVITY 2.1

Write out a deductive argument using premises and conclusions from a practice example.

What are the inferences or assumptions?

COMMENT

Doing this should allow you to see how much an argument relies on its inferences to make the links between the premises. As a deductive argument works from very general premises to more specific ones, it relies on a large number of inferences and assumptions which are naturally implicit. They obviously need to be made explicit, and examined and questioned further to see if they are correct and relevant. In our example, what has been proven in relation to ADHD and its impact on academic performance? Has drug X been tested with children of John's age?

Inductive arguments
An inductive argument usually argues and infers from the specific to the general, i.e. in the opposite way to a deductive argument. An inductive argument is one where the premises provide some evidence for the truth of the conclusion. Inductive arguments are not valid or invalid. This means that if the premises are true in an inductive argument, it is probable that the conclusion is true, but it might not be. Inductive reasoning consists of implying from the properties of a sample to the properties of a population as a whole and works with the notion of probabilities.

For example, suppose we have a container containing 1,000 beads. Some of the beads are red and some of the beads are blue. If we take a sample of 100 beads from the container and 50 of them are red and 50 of them are blue, then we could infer inductively that half the beads in the container are red and half are blue. In all probability we are likely to be about right, but we could also be very wrong. Inductive reasoning also depends on the similarity of the sample and the population. The more similar the sample is to the population as a whole, the more reliable will be the inductive implication. No inductive implication is perfect and any of them can fail. So, even though the premises are true, the conclusion might be false. Nonetheless, a good inductive implication will give us reason to believe that the conclusion is probably true.

Many general medical and social work theories are based upon observations of very specific experiments with samples. In our deductive example, one of the premises was based on such a theory: 'Drug X reduces hyperactivity in school children.' However, as we know, experiments cannot take into account all circumstances or situations (i.e. the evidence is incomplete). To see if this was an acceptable inductive conclusion in its own right, it would be necessary to see whether the experiments with drug X were tested with a similar sample of children to John and in relation to academic performance.

In an historical context, Bowlby's findings (1951,1969) suggested that infants who were separated from their mothers at an early age had behavioural and emotional difficulties later. This was used to argue the case against mothers working outside the home. This conclusion no doubt suited the economic conditions at the time; however, the data was based on children in very extreme institutionalised situations and one could argue that these were not 'typical' children. So the conclusion may not have been justified even though the research was accurate. Research usually progresses in this way with later researchers questioning aspects such as whether the sample was representative or whether the research contained assumptions invisible at the time (Cottrell, 2003).

ACTIVITY 2.2

Do you know of any theories that have been based on inductive reasoning?

Why are they considered valid?

COMMENT

The validity of any theory is considered in more detail later in this chapter, but any inductively based theory would need to have undergone further research to show its ongoing relevance and use for a wider population from the one where it was generated.

Abductive arguments

Another type of logic is called abductive reasoning where a person notes and/or observes a surprising circumstance and then develops the hypothesis that makes that circumstance a matter of course. It works from a description of something to a hypothesis that accounts for the reliable data within that description and seeks to explain relevant evidence. This 'good guessing' is based on what limited data is available at a given time, but it can be extended to encompass additional detailed testing and rigorous observation.

For example, you could get up in the morning and see that your lawn is very wet. If it rained last night, it would be unsurprising that the lawn is wet. So by abductive reasoning the possibility that it rained last night is a reasonable hypothesis. Another condition is also necessary here – the hypothesis should not just be sufficient but also the most economical or simplest explanation. So if you reasoned instead that aliens landed and sprayed your lawn with something that looked wet, that would not be an economical explanation and be classed as unsound abductive reasoning. Simplification and economy in an argument is a good rule of thumb, but we could also ask whether in a complicated medical or socially complex situation it is sometimes also necessary to look for a less obvious explanation.

Knowledge of critical thinking standards

Once the concepts (the ideas and language) of critical thinking are understood, we need standards that will enable us to deliberate and judge effectively and in a sound manner. Standards of critical analysis and appraisal are specific for each area of activity, i.e. standards for criticising an argument will be different from those used for criticising a piece of research.

Critical thinking standards do not always guide a thinker on how to apply them. Their nature makes it necessary for the critical thinker to exercise judgement in interpreting them and determining what they require in any particular case – which is how it should be if you think about it! The way in which you exercise this judgement and interpret the relevant standards gives you important material for discussion. The worst way to use them would be as unexamined tick-box lists. Developing such judgement is like learning a language – you don't follow an exact set of rules in speech, but you can act in a way the standards suggest (e.g. using unambiguous words and short sentences) and recognise when your thinking fulfils these relevant standards (e.g. other people understanding you, rules of grammar).

This is obviously a huge subject, so we have initially collated below the generalised standards relevant for the critical appraisal of deductive and inductive arguments. Further standards and principles for other aspects of professional practice, e.g. critically thinking about practical arguments, knowledge and reflection, are considered in later chapters. All these standards and principles obviously need to be kept under review to ensure they are appropriate for each particular context.

REFLECTION POINT

Where do you hear or make 'logical arguments' in the workplace?

Which standards or guiding principles do you apply to critically appraise them?

Have you come across any flawed reasoning or assumptions recently? How did you recognise and/or question them?

Critical analysis of deductive arguments (from Gibbs and Gambrill, 1999)

- Does the conclusion have at least one premise in support of it?
- Are all the premises relevant to the truth of the conclusion? A premise is only acceptable if it:

  - is a matter of undisputed common knowledge;
  - can be adequately defended;
  - is the conclusion of another sound argument;
  - is an incontrovertible eyewitness testimony;
  - is an incontrovertible report from an expert in the field;
  - is different from the conclusion itself;
  - does not contradict the evidence, a well-established claim, a reliable source or other premises in the same argument;
  - is not self-contradictory, linguistically confusing or unintelligible.

- When viewed together, do the premises constitute sufficient grounds for the truth of the conclusion? (i.e. strong enough in number, weight and kind – small and/or unrepresentative samples, or anecdotal evidence would be considered weak).
- Do the premises provide an effective rebuttal to all reasonable challenges to the argument? This is a good criterion for distinguishing mediocre arguments, because many people ignore or hide contrary evidence. Good arguers examine counter-arguments as well as compatible ones.

A deductive argument may be unsound because:

- there may be something wrong with its logical structure, e.g. when the conclusion does not follow on logically from the reasons preceding it and the inferences are weak;
- it contains 'false' (irrelevant, unacceptable, weak) premises;
- it bases conclusions on too little evidence (generalising from incomplete information) or overlooks alternative conclusions.

Critical analysis of inductive arguments

- The size of the sample should not be too small to support the conclusion.
- The sample used should not be relevantly different from the population as a whole.
- Any analogies between samples and population must be valid. (For example, it may be argued that since A has property P, so also B must have property P. The analogy fails when the two objects, A and B, are different in a way which affects whether they both have property P.)
- Important evidence which would undermine an inductive argument should not be excluded from consideration. The requirement that all relevant information be included is called the 'principle of total evidence'.

Knowledge of strategies

People discover or devise key strategies and procedures for guiding and critically checking their performance in a variety of thinking tasks, e.g. making lists of pros and cons for decision-making; using examples for clarifying terms; useful rules of thumb; discussing issues with a knowledgeable person. Specific strategies tend to be more helpful than those designed to apply in all cases and each of us will have our own preferred methods and techniques. What is most helpful is when they are made more explicit and shared among people struggling with the same issue.

ACTIVITY 2.3

List some strategies or tips you already have for practice, e.g. for making decisions, problem-solving; and for learning, e.g. reading, studying.

These ideas are great to share in groups – how can you create an opportunity to share ideas on your course or programme – over coffee, via e-mail?

COMMENT

Informal methods can be very successful ways to share ideas and ways of working with colleagues and team members, but it can also be productive to create a time within a more formal gathering so that more people can get involved.

Habits of mind

As Bailin et al. (1999, p294) point out, having all the intellectual resources necessary for critical thinking does not make anyone a critical thinker. The final resource is probably the most important of them all. We need to have certain commitments, attitudes or habits (e.g. respect for reason and truth, a truly open rather than a defensive attitude) and recognise the value of critical thinking in fostering true belief and responsible judgement/action as well. These attributes are closely tied up with our ethics and values. In Wilkins and Boahen's view (2013, p6) all social work practitioners need to *develop an 'analytical mindset' that pervades their practice in all areas*. Health and social work, with their interdisciplinary natures and inherent value system guiding judgement and action, are obviously well placed for fostering such habits of mind, but it is easy to become complacent and believe they are occurring automatically. In addition, of course, the ability of an organisation and a team to create conducive learning cultures aimed at encouraging and supporting such habits of mind is crucial here, a point we will return to in the following chapter. Chapter 7 looks more closely at how routine practice easily becomes uncritical, defensive and even arrogant within certain work environments.

In practice we need knowledge about the subject at hand, self-knowledge (an honest recognition of how we think and reason, and the biases we are prone to) plus a range of values, attitudes and dispositions related to personal humility, human rights and the dignity and intrinsic worth of all human beings. These attributes underpin the ability to practise critically and encourage the inherent requirements of social work: openness, questioning and responsibility.

REFLECTION POINT

Which specific professional values do you think are relevant to your critical thinking?

Review

We have chosen to use one set of critical thinking ideas to develop in this section but you will probably find other authors' work echoing this material. For example, Smith (1992) identifies three key factors in critical thinking: knowledge, authority and a willingness to doubt. 'Knowledge' fits exactly with our first intellectual resource of background knowledge; 'authority' would involve the use of our critical concepts, standards and strategies; and 'a willingness to doubt' would be our habit of mind.

As we can see, critical thinking cannot be thought of as something that finds perfect solutions. Rather, the skills and abilities of critical thinking allow the best quality decisions or actions possible for the situations we encounter. Our holistic view advocates not just the application of critical thinking principles and techniques, but a more developed understanding of how our thinking operates in our day-to-day environments and the dangers we need to become more aware of.

We have only focused on more formal arguments in this chapter to initially demonstrate the usage of these ideas. However, your own learning will provide many opportunities to use these critical thinking principles in undertaking professional judgement, using new knowledge in practice, in reflecting on learning and practice and when writing. We will now explore each of these areas in turn in the following chapters and develop the notion of critical thinking within them.

FURTHER READING

Brookfield, S (1987) *Developing critical thinkers.* Milton Keynes: Open University Press.

A general but insightful look at becoming a critical person.

Fisher, A (2001) *Critical thinking: An introduction.* Cambridge: Cambridge University Press.

An excellent introduction for specific critical thinking concepts and techniques.

Jones-Devitt, S and Smith, L (2007) *Critical thinking in health and social care.* London: Sage.

A range of different approaches can be found in this text that help explore a wider view of critical thinking.

Moon, J (2008) *Critical thinking: An exploration of theory and practice.* London: Routledge.

This book provides a series of ideas from the literature as well as very practical advice.

Wilkins, D and Boahen, G (2013) *Critical analysis skills for social workers.* Maidenhead: Open University Press/McGraw Hill Education.

This text offers a step-by-step model for developing an analytical mindset.

The Critical Thinking Community: www.criticalthinking.org

The Foundation and Center for Critical Thinking aim to improve education in US colleges, universities and primary through to secondary schools.

Chapter 3
Professional judgement

Professional judgement is a crucial aspect in the development of professional expertise. Prescribed procedures are an important and necessary feature of practice, and they can deal well with typical scenarios. However, they can be found to prove inadequate guidance for new and unusual situations because they are incomplete in two key ways. First, they do not encompass the judgement necessary to critically apply them and take account of specific circumstances. Second, they are also unable to encompass the more tacit skills, knowledge and capabilities which make up professional judgement and expertise. In Dunne's (2011, pp16–17) explanation, when practice is reduced to a technical procedure it is through the abstraction of a 'rational core' – an explicit general formula that can be replicated and controlled. The problem is that this *entails disembedding the knowledge implicit in the skilful performance of the characteristic tasks of the practice from the immediacy and idiosyncrasy of the particular situations in which it is deployed, and from the experience and character in the practitioners in whom it resides.* In effect, it becomes a *practitioner-proof mode of practice.* Unfortunately, some organisations or teams exhibit a 'command-and-control' culture where procedural reliance has become dominant. However, it is within the context of a more open 'learning culture' where practitioners may have the freedom to develop and use their expertise and judgement in providing a more tailored and/or creative response within any necessary prescribed guidelines (Thompson, 2006).

An important point to note here is that for effective professional judgements to be made and have an appropriate impact, there also needs to be clear, value-based leadership exhibited by all practitioners. Cases of systematic abuse of vulnerable people as discussed in the Francis Report (2013) show the need for a clear sense of personal responsibility and professional leadership. The well-known phrase 'all that is necessary for the triumph of evil is for good men to do nothing' comes to mind. Without clear moral leadership based on professional judgement, values and standards, a culture can develop where abusive behaviour is left unchallenged and becomes tolerated. Professional, moral judgement is clearly not in evidence in these situations. The key point we are trying to make here is that high quality professional practice encompasses individual leadership based on sound judgement derived from a set of professional moral standards. Every professional can take a lead to ensure that not only is best possible practice fostered but a working climate is also developed within which all those involved in care are clear that abusive practices in any form will not be tolerated.

ACTIVITY 3.1

Note the range of professional judgements you make in practice. Which are prescribed by organisational procedure and to what extent?

COMMENT

This could obviously be a long list! It is interesting to note just how much of our own thinking, interpretation, reasoning and decision-making is necessary to put policies, procedures and day-to-day processes into practice, no matter how 'prescribed' they are. Of course, such judgement is underpinned by the enactment of our morals and values.

Professional judgement is associated with accountable decision-making as well as risk assessment and management, and therefore with the ability to predict the future and manage risk of harm. Obviously, there has to be a realistic expectation of professionals' abilities to make predictions about future harm and manage such risk. Such decisions are, and will always be, fallible because human beings are essentially unpredictable – we cannot eradicate risk, only reduce the probability of harm. In both healthcare (Standing, 2010) and social work (Taylor, 2013) the professional judgement process has to be based on realistic conceptions of human strengths and weaknesses, work with uncertainty and be as sound and robust as it can be. Indeed, any managerial or leadership decision-making has to try to achieve this, and one way is to ensure the process is not only value-based but also openly subject to critical thinking. This, in turn, needs to avoid a prescriptive approach to practice, and focus on professional learning and increasing capability and expertise.

To take account of these issues in particular fields of practice we would refer you to the Further Reading at the end of the chapter as a useful starting point. For this text we concentrate on an important but general aspect of professional judgement that can now be identified and explored in more detail – practical reasoning.

Practical reasoning

Recent literature (e.g. Bondi et al., 2011; Kinsella and Pitman, 2012) notes the continuing relevance of the concept of *phronesis*, which is Aristotle's notion of practical moral wisdom, to our current need to define legitimate knowledge and processes within professional decision-making. Judgement is said to be at the core of professional practice, and it is practical reasoning which is said to be a key part of this judgement-making process (Kondrat, 1992; Beckett and Hager, 2001; Kinsella and Pitman, 2012).

Of course, ethical reasoning is also a vital part of health and social work decision-making, and there is an important ethical and moral aspect to practical reasoning which we will address briefly first. In practice, there are numerous ethical dilemmas being faced every day – for example, balancing the right to self-determination against risk of harm, dealing with budget cuts or reforms that compromise service quality and meeting complex needs of service users within a strict legal or target-based framework. Some may be covered by applying set ethical standards and principles to guide practice; for others, a personal value base may have to be referred to. In essence, critical thinking comes into play in a number of ways, e.g. making sure our own values are explicit and appropriate, understanding the ethics and values of our profession and its legal/statutory framework, as well as maintaining a person-centred approach and professional accountability, of course – but a full exploration of this topic is seen to be beyond the scope of this handbook at the present time. We refer you to several useful texts in the Further Reading section at the end of the chapter.

Making professional judgements, and the practical wisdom and reasoning this involves, appears central to the idea of professionalism and reflective practice in general. It is about *working out how to act suitably in the face of ambiguity without preset formulae or highly detailed plans of action . . . combining knowledge, judgement, understanding and intuition* (Macklin and Whiteford, 2012, p92). Logical reasoning and arguments (seen in the previous chapter) are not dismissed, but the use of reason in a formalised, logical or theoretical sense (i.e. to decide what to believe) is not necessarily sufficient to decide what to actually do in a certain situation. Practical reasoning, because it is the use of reason directed towards action, helps determine how to figure out what to do and how to do it (Streumer, 2009).

We must be very clear that this is not about procedural problems where requirements are already established and the problem defined. Practical reasoning is not a mathematical or logical calculation and there are no determinate answers (Ellett, 2012). Practical deliberation involves the effective use of a wide range of knowledge and information to understand problems, define areas within which solutions can be sought and justify the arguments and judgements that guided the choice between possible solutions. It activates, critically appraises and interprets formal and informal knowledge, skills, attributes and values to this end.

In effect, it is about the desirability of certain actions from a professional's point of view. A sign of professional maturity is a shift away from decisions that are arbitrated by an external authority to one in which individuals provide their own justification for decisions, using their own as well as others' expertise or requirements (Kandlbinder, 2007). This aligns well with the fundamental essence of professional judgement – making sure the most sound and moral option is produced for the situation at hand, and taking responsibility for that.

Practical reasoning works by encouraging an informed, explicit, moral and reasonable relationship between situational goals and actions; it therefore promotes a critically reflective, reciprocal dialogue between those means and ends. It also promotes an interaction between the general rules and knowledge that guide practice with the ability to discern the unique characteristics of a situation (Hibbert, 2012). This is a key feature for health and social work, and indeed for any people-based profession (Bondi et al., 2011).

One fundamental feature of practical reasoning is that there is no established process to it because it is happening in active, complex and evolving or uncertain situations. Practical reasoning, therefore, cannot be viewed or approached as a prescriptive list of rules to be followed, and if it starts to establish too set a path or imposes regulatory systems it becomes rigid and unworkable (Sellman, 2012). Nevertheless, there are particular features and principles associated with practical reasoning. It is important that these are understood in order to make practical reasoning as good as it can be, and to allow an objective and critical evaluation of it where possible or necessary, i.e. apply a critical thinking approach to it. Of course, there are never any guarantees for a good outcome and it also needs to be acknowledged that uncertainty can never be avoided or overcome, but it can be acknowledged and worked with constructively. Table 3.1 presents the principles of sound practical reasoning that allow this. The key principle is the first because the basis of practical wisdom resides in the *preparedness to understand a given situation in different ways and not to accept immediately that a situation is what it appears to be* (Kemmis, 2012, p155). This theme of understanding the situation and its complexity is reiterated throughout the framework. Other aspects cover the critical use of theoretical and informal knowledge, cognitive skills and the ethical basis of professional discernment and judgement-making.

Table 3.1 Framework of practical reasoning principles

Practical reasoning principles
Situational appreciation – i.e. sensitivity to, and discernment of, the particular characteristics and features of a situation (including ethics, circumstances and needs).
Attention paid to the complexity and uncertainty of a situation – i.e. this is not ignored or overly reduced.
Transparent purpose and intentions – e.g. explicable aims/objectives.
Critical appraisal and interpretation of formal and informal knowledge, skills, attributes and values.
A clear exchange between the particular characteristics and features of the situation (e.g. a person's behaviour) and the wider context (e.g. social/cultural norms) in order to gain a fully informed view, as well as between subjective (personal) and objective (neutral) perspectives.
A moral and reasonable relationship is established between goals/objectives and resulting decisions/actions via a critically reflective, reciprocal dialogue between means (how we do something) and ends (the outcome).
Critical thinking is used within the process to: • weigh up risks, options, pros and cons, contingencies;   • adjudicate between competing goals and demands;   • generate and deliberate between alternatives, choices;   • create review or monitoring points;   • take into account relevant constraints and limitations.
Outcomes, decisions/actions are prudent, appropriate and useful to the situation's needs, etc.
New understanding and meaning (expertise) is developed.

ACTIVITY 3.2

Applying the principles

Think about a particular area of practice you have recently been involved with where you exercised your judgement. Use the details of this situation to make notes under each of the principles above, and see how useful they are to help examine and explore your practical reasoning and the judgement you made.

COMMENT

The principles can highlight important aspects of understanding and working with situations in a rigorous way, but we can be restricted by the amount of time and information available to us – it will never be perfect! Nevertheless, becoming aware of the principles of sound practical reasoning can not only enable us to review and improve the information and processes we are working with, but also help us to recognise when the information or processes are inadequate, and when we need to delay making a decision. This framework can therefore become a useful reflective tool.

Further critical thinking about practical reasoning

As well as using the principles detailed above to understand and critically review practical reasoning, there are other significant underpinning issues to be aware of. The first is that deciding what to do, or what the 'best' thing is to do, will be greatly influenced by the presumptions, preconceptions and 'givens' within the situation, which, as ever, become hidden biases and prejudices being worked to. These may relate to local or national strategies or rhetoric, to organisational constraints or to more personal beliefs. Posing critical 'trigger' questions right from the start can help us unearth and examine them before they exert their influence too strongly. A critical awareness of why what we have thought of as the best option is 'best' should be made explicit. The overall point is to raise awareness of aspects of ourselves, our team and our organisations and culture that are usually subconscious but which have the power to impact heavily on our thought processes and our more conscious reasoning, decisions and actions.

Brookfield (2012) views assumptions within three different categories:

- causal/predictive – 'if I/you do this . . . then that will happen';

- prescriptive – desirable ways to behave/think; relate to values etc. – 'I/you should/ ought to do this';

- paradigmatic – deeply held ways we frame the world, e.g. ideology, culture, beliefs – 'This is right'.

The easiest way to view this is to understand how the last category informs the rest. The movement from the idea of institutionalisation to one of helping people live independent lives has been a major shift in the way we view and accept what 'best' care is for vulnerable members of society. However, this underlying viewpoint will restrict any thinking about a situation in significant ways by providing an existing frame for it that allows certain outcomes (i.e. staying in the family home) to be more 'acceptable' or 'right' than others. In a different example, a social worker may not take notes during a meeting with a client because:

- paradigmatic assumption: social work is a non-oppressive culture;

- prescriptive assumption: I should show I am not oppressive . . . ;

- causal assumption: if I don't take notes I will be able to listen more and make eye contact etc. and so not appear oppressive . . .

The social worker's behaviour and actions are being directed by that initial paradigmatic assumption. Sometimes these assumptions can be completely unconscious; at other times we can be aware of them and refer back to them for underpinning guidance as our value base, but most of the time they are left unquestioned. The key issue is that the client could easily interpret the social worker's action very differently, i.e. they may not feel oppressed but if they were expecting the social worker to take notes (because to them that shows interest and respect), then they could feel very devalued. If you are a health worker we are sure you will be able to reflect on similar situations that arise where patients have felt devalued by particular systems or processes that are well-intentioned but become inflexible barriers to care.

REFLECTION POINT

Which critical 'trigger' questions might help uncover the 'givens' within a situation?

This is not an easy task but the need is to expose what is already understood, accepted, perceived or expected. It will be more effective, therefore, if someone else questions us and plays 'devil's advocate' to determine the existence and validity of these positions. Our need is to question and think critically enough about what impact our behaviour and actions might have on others who would not have the same paradigmatic starting point.

An associated issue is that we usually have limited and/or imperfect information to work with. This obviously affects our ability to achieve the necessary situational awareness which underpins effective practical reasoning. Establishing a critical awareness of what information or understanding might be lacking can be a key part of the learning involved in any situation; looking at how to address such deficiency in the future increases the potential for developing further expertise.

Judgement statements

In practice we may also be called on to make quick judgement calls, or a brief summary of a situation in the form of statements. These types of statements can be defined and explored briefly here to understand their nature and critically consider them.

It may be that the type of language we are using is not suitable for the impact or outcome needed, or we may wish to challenge someone else's statements.

Here are some brief examples.

- *John is not in the right type of environment.* A value statement – values are different for everyone and so what the 'right' type of environment is would need to be made explicit and critically examined.

- *John has injuries.* An empirical statement – these injuries should be in evidence and are therefore verifiable. However, how and why they were sustained would need further detail to clearly establish any further implication here.

- *John is unhappy.* A conceptual statement – because concepts are ideas that relate to a class of objects, they are not specific. More detailed or empirical 'evidence' is needed to verify and make explicit what is meant.

- *John will be subject to more abuse if we do not act.* A causal statement – assumes one thing affects another but the detail of the more specific connection and cause is missing.

Establishing professional authority

Until recently, professional judgement and practical reasoning have perhaps not been given the full appreciation and value they deserve within formal health or social work practice and education. They may have been viewed as too tacit, practice-based or subjective, and inadvertently ignored in favour of a reliance on authority from external sources, e.g. theory or research as justification for decisions and/or actions. Cameron (2009, p11) notes this *deeply embedded [knowledge] hierarchy inherent in the system*. It is hoped that professional judgement and practical reasoning can now become more explicit and examined as pivotal aspects of professional expertise. In our view it is sound practical reasoning that provides at least part of the necessary 'internal' authority and justification for establishing sound professional judgement. The principles detailed above in this chapter can be used as suitable evaluation criteria for professional development and learning, encompassing as they do the necessary abilities for sound reasoning and deliberation with knowledge, skills and values in practical situations.

Indeed, it can be seen that practical reasoning underpins and informs professional deliberation and judgement across a wide range of dilemmas concerning what to do and how to it. To return to the example above, our reasoning could be:

- interpreting a colleague's notes on John, or the latest theory on child development to explore John's situation more fully;

- working out which piece of research is the most valid and appropriate for better understanding John's behaviour;

- considering the best way to communicate with John and his family;

- deciding whether or not John needs to be removed from his family.

In these deliberations we can develop a robust ability to make sound judgements by making best critical use of our own expertise, as well as the expertise of others, in a clear and moral relationship with the situation at hand. It is this moral relationship between means and ends which is provided by practical reasoning. In becoming aware of this reasoning and deliberation as much as we can, and seeking to improve it, we are cultivating the judgement and authority which is at the heart of professional practice development.

Review

This chapter has focused on some relevant aspects and processes of professional judgement, in particular practical reasoning, to show how critical thinking can help inform and enhance them. As professional judgement is at the heart of expertise and informs specific areas of practice such as leadership, decision-making and risk assessment, it is an area where critical consideration is crucial in establishing professional authority and in maintaining safe and accountable practice.

As we have seen, professional judgement and deliberation is applied to a wide range of deliberations and decisions in practice. The use of new knowledge in practice is one such key area and is the subject of the next chapter.

FURTHER READING

Banks, S (2012) *Ethics and values in social work.* 4th edition. London: Palgrave Macmillan.

Bondi, L, Carr, D, Clark, C and Clegg, C (eds) (2011) *Towards professional wisdom: Practical deliberation in the people professions.* Farnham: Ashgate.

This collection of key authors from different professional fields critically discusses the notions of professional judgement, wisdom and deliberation.

Kinsella, EA and Pitman, A (eds) (2012) *Phronesis as professional knowledge: Practical wisdom in the professions.* Rotterdam: Sense Publishers.

Phronesis is Aristotle's notion of practical, moral wisdom – an idea that is explored by a number of authors from health and education fields in order to re-examine professional knowledge, practical reasoning and judgement.

O'Sullivan, T (2010) *Decision making in social work.* 2nd edition. London: Macmillan.

A new edition which provides a supportive framework for making social work judgements and assessments based on a structured and practical approach.

Standing, M (2010) *Clinical judgement and decision making in nursing and interprofessional healthcare.* Maidenhead: McGraw Hill, Open University Press.

This text covers the knowledge, skills, values and process of clinical judgement and decision-making and provides useful reflective activities.

Taylor, B (2013) *Professional decision making and risk in social work.* 2nd edition. London: Sage/Learning Matters.

Provides guidance and help for social work practitioners and students to make professional decisions with clients, from exercising statutory powers and duties to protect children from abuse, to making decisions about risk.

Chapter 4
Using knowledge in practice

Qualifying and CPD learning will introduce you to a range of formal knowledge such as policy, legislation, theory and research in the specialist area of your choice.

We have seen in the previous chapter that professional judgement uses knowledge to help inform deliberations about what to do – practical reasoning activates and interprets a wide range of formal and informal knowledge, skills and values to this end. We can also see that the principles of practical reasoning help us undertake sound, moral reasoning and deliberation with knowledge in practical situations. In other words, we use knowledge when making professional judgements, but such use of knowledge involves professional judgement and critical thinking in its own right. This use of knowledge in practice will be an active and important learning experience because any knowledge cannot always be applied systematically or predictably to work situations, and things won't necessarily go according to plan. It will be an interpretive and iterative process. Developing practice in this way, by putting into use new ideas and knowledge, is one of the most important ways critical thinking can be practised in the workplace (Argyris and Schön, 1974).

Critical use of formal knowledge in practice

If we look at these processes more closely, we can see that formal knowledge (such as theory and research findings) can only inform practice; it cannot predict or control exactly what will take place. Theoretical methods, models and frameworks that explain the world we are in, what practice is and how to do it, as well as research evidence, is extremely useful material for any professional (especially those who are newly qualified). They help us gain more information and understanding about the issues as well as possible interventions and outcomes, but they cannot be taken 'off the shelf' as an unmediated solution. In fact, it would be difficult to reduce the complex, uncertain and unstable situations we work with to something that a standardised theoretical body of knowledge, or a set of specific research findings, can answer (Adams et al., 2009).

The way we deal with new knowledge can follow a process which aligns with the way we 'learn'. Learning is usually about fitting new material into existing material; dealing with new knowledge usually involves the processes of abstracting general principles from the new ideas so that they can be matched with, or connected to, the knowledge we already have (Sotto, 1994). Some of the original ideas, rules or procedures from this knowledge may remain relatively intact during this process, but the process itself produces new understanding. As Race (2001) puts it, the abstracting of principles or generalising involves a lot of 'digesting':

- sorting out what is important;
- extracting fundamental principles;
- discarding what is not important;
- establishing a sense of ownership of it.

For practical use this knowledge will need to be interpreted and adapted further for the specific and unique conditions of any situation, and integrated with experience and values as well. In terms of practical reasoning this aligns with the situational appreciation and discernment necessary to ensure a moral and reasonable relationship between aims and outcomes. The justification for something being done or decided on is not made on the inherent authority of a theory or a piece of research (although their reliability and credibility is obviously important), but on the professional judgement (the reasoning, deliberation and decisions) that analysed and evaluated the information for a specific purpose. As Dunne (2011, p18) explains, *professional judgement involves the ability to actuate knowledge with relevance, appropriateness, or sensitivity to the context.*

There is no model or process for how formal knowledge is mediated to make it relevant and useful – such a transfer of knowledge is not an exact or linear process, but as practitioners we are constantly building on and using our inputs of information and knowledge whether we are fully aware of it or not. Mathews and Crawford's (2011) text provides an excellent guide to the critical use and development of knowledge in social work that is also transferable to other contexts, supporting the view that an organic, evolving relationship between practice and knowledge is desirable.

ACTIVITY 4.1

Think about a particular theory you use a lot in practice, or one that underpins your overall approach – note the ways it has helped you understand a situation or decide what to do. Do you understand that theory differently now from when you first learnt about it? What are its strengths and its limitations?

COMMENT

Using theory proactively means interpreting it, but also understanding how and why it is useful for each situation. This process will necessarily show up any limitations in the scope or depth of the theory, but you will probably understand the theory and your practice more by doing this. This is a creative process because you will be using your own experience and understanding, plus other formal or informal knowledge, to extend and adapt the theory as necessary as well. In effect, new knowledge for your practice is created and it is important to be critically aware of where your position is now, and why.

Using new knowledge gained from an academic environment for practice can at first be conscious and deliberative. There are a number of difficulties. As seen earlier, the authority of theory and research can be viewed as unchallengeable wisdom. To criticise this type of knowledge might seem presumptuous, but it is important to show how knowledge meant for practice can be used for specific situations and how it actually 'performs' when used. By starting to use judgement with this knowledge in particular cases with appropriate support and guidance (e.g. in supervision), newly qualified practitioners can develop their confidence, expertise and their own professional authority. In effect, the holistic and interdependent nature of the social work Professional Capabilities Framework can be used here to encourage such thinking across the various domains, e.g. applying knowledge (Domain 5) critically (Domain 6) and ethically (Domain 2) to make appropriate decisions (Domain 7) with others (Domain 8) to promote well-being (Domain 4) and recognise diversity (Domain 3) can show professionalism (Domain 1) and leadership (Domain 9).

However, newly qualified practitioners may be more comfortable working with formal, external knowledge rather than more personal knowledge because they do not have an established and evaluated frame of reference built upon experience to create a sense of confidence in what they know. Use of formal knowledge can then follow a deductive process, i.e. working from the generalised aspects of known theories and frameworks, or research findings, and mechanistically applying them to a particular situation. The issue here is that these ideas may be imposed on new situations in order to understand them, and the inherent meaning of the situation (usually contained within the detail) may be lost when trying to produce rational solutions. In effect, the situation may become manipulated to fit the template of the theory, which distorts true understanding. Instead, Margetson (2000, cited Nixon and Murr, 2006, p807) advocates an inductive approach, where reasoning is developed first from observed (or simulated/reproduced) examples with reference back to formal knowledge. This enables more interpretive habits and develops a practitioner's professional judgement, confidence and authority, and in turn allows for the complexity of the situation to be taken into account.

From a critical thinking perspective the process of using new knowledge in practice may require a framework to ensure certain activities are covered, which provides the process with a necessary robustness and validity. In other words, we are trying to ensure that it is not merely a 'trial-and-error' exercise. Our framework for using new knowledge in practice (Table 4.1) is based on an inductive approach. It follows principles associated with practical reasoning and starts with an understanding of the practice situation. We have also aligned the process with useful evaluation and generic assessment criteria (QAAHE, 2008). Such a framework will help ensure that the process ultimately addresses situation-focused needs, but also allows you to demonstrate, evidence and evaluate the type of learning achieved.

Obviously, this process involves more than a straightforward or linear application of particular technical skills and is a highly reflective experience generating a practitioner's own knowledge for practice. Responsible assessment and deliberation will also be very apparent throughout the process, as well as other more implicit and less conscious elements – for example, perception, interpretation, emotion. It is, therefore,

Table 4.1 Framework for using new knowledge in practice with associated assessment criteria

Activities associated with using new knowledge in practice	Generic assessment criteria
A. Understand the situation's circumstances and needs, and your aims and objectives	Analysis, comprehension
B. Identify and evaluate relevant formal knowledge in respect of the above	Critical appraisal, evaluation
C. Combine principles with other knowledge, experience, ideas and values	Transformation of abstract data and concepts, synthesis
D. Use to inform or direct decisions and actions	Design, creativity, transfer
E. Critically monitor and judge new understanding and meaning	Evaluation

useful to undertake it in a supervised or mentored situation involving reflection. We will deal with the reflective element in a later chapter.

Critical appraisal of formal knowledge

If we revisit our set of 'intellectual resources' for critical thinking we can see various alignments when appraising formal knowledge. Overall, the framework presented above can be seen to provide a number of critical thinking strategies.

Standards for critical appraisal of theories (from Newman, 2000)

- According to this theory, what determines human behaviour?
- What are the major beliefs of the theory – which do I accept and why? Which don't I accept and why?
- Are the assumptions clearly defined; reasonable; ethically and socially consistent with my own and social work's assumptions and values?
- How applicable is the theory across settings, different clients and problems?
- Is the theory clear, easy to understand and logical?
- Does the theory address cultural, ethical or racial issues? Is it culturally sensitive?
- What is the empirical (testable) support for the theory?
- Is it original?
- How does the theory compare and contrast with other theoretical approaches?
- The main question has to be: does it apply in my situation – how and why?

Standards for critical appraisal of research evidence

The critical appraisal of research evidence requires some specialist training, but these questions should start you off.

- Have the authors clearly explained the purpose of the study, how it was carried out and the results?

- How confident can we be that the study sample is representative of the broader population – or does it relate to my clients?

- Did some people 'drop out' of the study and, if so, have the authors accounted for this in their conclusions?

- Have the authors showed how the findings were 'worked out'? How far are they generalising from a small sample?

- Have the authors any reason to be biased?

- Are the claims made by the study plausible?

- Does the study add anything to what we already know?

- The main question has to be: does it apply in my situation – how and why?

ACTIVITY 4.2

Identify a particularly complex issue from practice. What else do you need to know or understand about it? Now form an 'enquiry question' by asking yourself 'why?', i.e. 'What aspect of my practice could be improved'; 'What will this improved knowledge or understanding help me to achieve?' Search for and identify a theory, a model, a discussion or recent research evidence associated with this issue. Apply the standards above as appropriate – in particular, the final question in each list should be expanded with your own enquiry question to help you evaluate the relevance of the new knowledge or evidence for your specific development needs.

COMMENT

The underlying need to use new knowledge to understand a particular issue should help to direct and guide your appraisal of it in a more focused way (i.e. rather than doing it as a purely academic exercise). As you start to analyse knowledge in respect of your own question, you critically engage with it with a defined purpose, but you may also need to reword your initial question and/or make it more generalised. Our practice-based questions can be too specific and too focused on looking for a specific 'answer' that we think is 'out there'. As we have seen in the previous chapter, developing our practice should be about understanding an issue and its context better, and then forming our own answers. For example, asking 'How do I talk to someone with a learning disability?' can be reformed to a more generic and open, user-centred question: 'What are the main communication issues for people with learning needs?' The improved understanding gained from asking this question of the literature can then better inform our practical reasoning and deliberation, plus the development of an 'answer' that is more suitable for the context and its needs.

Developing new understanding and practice-based knowledge

The inductive approach, therefore, creates a reinterpretation of meaning in new contexts rather than imposition of one truth across contexts. For Fook et al. (2000, p191) this becomes 'contextual theory development', which we can call the production of practice-based knowledge. Lester (1995) has previously argued that it is no longer adequate to base professional development on transmitting existing knowledge or developing a predefined range of competences. He wants practitioners to be able to construct and reconstruct the knowledge and skills they need and continually evolve their practice, in order to respond intelligently to unknown situations and go beyond established knowledge to create unique interpretations and outcomes. His ideas combine the notions of practical reasoning and professional judgement with the use and creation of practice-based knowledge. The expert 'skill' lies in being able to theorise the situation first in order to construct the problem to be solved. Key tools are analysis, synthesis, situational and ethical understanding, the ability to interpret the meanings of situations from a range of perspectives, as well as analytical and critical use of formal knowledge. What we have as a result is not a reduced concept of professional expertise but an appreciation of the divergent but also holistic, interconnected and value-based nature of situations and problems.

The creation of such professional knowledge from practice echoes even earlier work by Schön (1983) and Eraut (1994), who advocate the support and guidance of practitioners through experience to understand and determine the value of this knowledge, and to critically evaluate the development of practice-based theories. A review (Nixon and Murr, 2006) of thinking in this area for social work practice has concluded that professional knowledge is created by a practitioner by combining and recombining more explicit theoretical knowledge with an understanding of tacit or implicit knowledge from professional processes. This legitimate generation of practice-based knowledge can take fuller account of the complexity and uncertainty of practice. In this respect, professional knowledge becomes more holistic and concerned with 'being' rather than just knowing, and thus necessarily complex and extensive.

We can also see that this practice-based knowledge, once legitimately generated and evaluated, can become potent material for CPD learning. The articulation of such knowledge within supervision, assignments and portfolios creates the necessary confidence and 'voice' from which to argue and reason more coherently and robustly. This is explored in more detail in Chapter 6. It also works towards a clearer understanding of a practitioner's or even a team's 'theories in use' (Argyris and Schön, 1974).

Although many practitioners see their practice-based knowledge as intuitive and personal, and therefore unworthy of acknowledgement in an academic environment, it does not have to lack the rigour, testability or validity of academic knowledge if we can demonstrate critical awareness, validation and evaluation of it. Eraut (1994) in particular stated that professional education should not ignore the knowledge embedded in application and practice, and more recently Clark (2011) states that there is an increasing recognition of the power and legitimacy of practice knowledge in professional communities. Learning or developing practice knowledge can involve haphazard and unplanned processes. But practice is not necessarily idiosyncratic or implicit. Whatever is consciously and intentionally performed as practice implies an underpinning set of principles being acted upon. These principles will usually be based upon theoretical knowledge, experience, as well as values, and are at the heart of the notion of expertise. We can also add that sound practical reasoning will contribute a critical robustness to the process.

The main point is that many of these principles can be explored and evidenced by identifying and appraising the processes and content of our practical reasoning and actions. In fact, to be totally unaware of them would be tantamount to not taking responsibility for the effects of our actions, which is unacceptable in any profession. As professional knowledge depends on the range of contexts in which it is used and tested, we can begin to create powerful meanings from our accumulated experience for the purposes of CPD learning. For many students the process of identifying, articulating and evaluating their practice-based knowledge has been a very empowering learning experience because they have begun to discover their own voice.

However, the articulation of developing practices may prove a challenge to those practitioners who have been out of formal education for a while. Trying to make our learning, experience and knowledge more explicit for CPD learning is a major undertaking. We need to take extra time to examine more closely what we do, why we do it and what this means. One way of dealing with this is to use reflection, which is the subject of the next chapter.

FURTHER READING

Fisher, T and Somerton, J (2000) Reflection on action: The process of helping social workers to develop their use of theory in practice. *Social Work Education*, 19 (4), 387–401.

This paper clarifies what integrating theory and practice actually means and also suggests a model for exploring the use of theory in practice for use in supervision.

Mathews, I and Crawford, K (2011) *Evidence-based practice in social work*. Exeter: Learning Matters.

A text that offers a critical approach to the debate concerning the reliability and validity of the evidence, research and knowledge that underpins professional social work practice.

Pawson, R, Boaz, A, Grayson, L, Long, A and Barnes, C (2003) *Types and quality of knowledge in social care*. Knowledge Review No. 3. London: SCIE.

This knowledge review identifies the main types of research, experience and wisdom that combine to form the social care knowledge base and proposes a framework for assessing the quality of knowledge of any type.

Webber, M (2015) *Applying research evidence in social work practice*. London: Palgrave Macmillan Education.

A useful introduction to the techniques and debates around evidence-based practice.

Chapter 5
Critical reflection

Critical thinking itself involves a reflective dimension and the idea of reflective learning is therefore closely connected to it (Brookfield, 1987). We may not always be sure about what reflection is (any more than we can fully understand what learning is) and Ixer (1999, 2010) in particular argues that we do not know enough about its processes to assess it validly. However, we can understand what it can do within our own context in encouraging accountability in practice, and we have already seen its place within practical reasoning and professional judgement.

Reflection is, therefore, a central aspect to ongoing learning and development. Being reflective will allow awareness, analysis and evaluation of these educational and practice-based experiences in order to fully realise and better express the knowledge gained, and the learning and development that took place. The way you do this is a crucial factor in your achievement. Emphasis is placed not on a descriptive account of what happened but on a full-scale examination of the hows, whys and 'what it all means' for future practice.

What is reflection?

When described in the literature critical reflection is usually referred to as the thinking activities engaged in to critically analyse and evaluate experiences, producing outcomes of new understandings and appreciations of the way we think and operate. The concept of self-awareness is always apparent within the associated concept of reflexivity, which allows the subjective element (personal beliefs, feelings and emotions) to be analysed and evaluated at the same time. The consideration of external knowledge to provide a broad and current context may also be included.

Schön (1983, 1987) developed ideas around two main types of reflection for practice.

- 'Reflection on action' – when we think back on something already done.
- 'Reflection in action' – when we think about what we are doing while we are doing it.

Even though he uses the same term it would seem apparent that the processes are very different. When we are doing something we rarely have the time or opportunity to be consciously deliberative or analytical about it, and so the manner of our 'reflection' is likely to be more holistic, intuitive and automatic in this latter situation (Van Manen, 1995).

For the former situation (reflection on action) we can think of reflection as a developing personal ability. Everyone seems to adopt their own method to help it happen: some people like to keep a journal, others make jottings or notes, some draw pictures or mind maps and others just think in the bath. To do it effectively there are some guidelines to follow, and deep and critical levels to achieve for CPD learning, and these will be explained below. In essence, all it takes is an ability to think, to be self-aware and to question – but it takes practice to develop a method suitable for you and attain the necessary level, as we don't always do this automatically. Practice needs time, commitment and some support – these are the variables.

What does it achieve?

Your reflection will produce a lot of thoughts, ideas, connections and insights into your learning and development. This also follows Schön's (1987) ideas that show how professional expertise is developed through the use of critical reflection. Rather than repeating the same experience or developing one's own implicit 'rules of thumb', etc., practitioners can explore, understand and justify their practice deliberations, reasoning, decisions and actions in different ways using critical intellectual resources, and develop new perspectives for future practice using available theory, research, knowledge and experience.

To use the earlier language of Argyris and Schön (1974), we reveal our 'theories-in-use' (the implicit theories that govern our actual behaviour and contain assumptions about self, others and environment) and examine them against our espoused theory (the words we use to convey what we do or what we would like others to think we do) to see if they fit. A small gap between the two might not be a bad thing but if it gets too wide, then there is clearly a difficulty. Provided the two remain connected, the gap creates a dynamic for reflection and for dialogue.

However, our need goes beyond being a reflective practitioner in a narrow sense. Because reflection for our purposes is in a social work and health education context, the main outcome of reflection is seen to be an identification and evaluation of the learning and development pertaining to future practice, i.e. the development of the self as a critical practitioner (Adams et al., 2009). The aim is to think beyond the acknowledgement and description of difficult aspects of a situation to an evaluation of how they were dealt with, i.e. the practical reasoning, judgement and resulting action, as well as their meaning and significance.

The overall standards of learning in this context therefore concern change and development. These ideas are discussed in more depth by Mezirow et al. (1990) as the development of practice to oppose and redress power imbalances. The main outcome of critical reflection on practice will therefore be an identification and evaluation of that learning and development relevant to values, as well as future practice methods.

Argyris and Schön (1974) call it 'double-loop learning' when an 'error' is detected and corrected in ways that involve the modification of underlying norms, values and objectives, as well as the techniques or strategies. In other words, we need not only to ask if we are doing things right, but also if we are doing the right thing, plus (for triple-loop learning) how did we decide (or have accepted) what is 'right' or 'best' in the first place. We explored this idea in Chapter 3 in relation to the assumptions underpinning and influencing our practical reasoning. These authors argue that double-loop learning at least is necessary if practitioners are to make informed decisions in rapidly changing and often uncertain contexts. This learning should also encompass and, if possible, inform policy changes at organisational level where appropriate.

How far do we go with reflection?

Kolb (1984), using earlier work by others including Rogers, Piaget and Lewin, further developed a model called the experiential learning cycle, where the learner is seen to move from being an active participant in an experience, to a reflector on it, to an analyst of it and then on to an experimenter with new ideas for a new experience. Reflective learning for us goes further to draw out the complete 'learning' for the person and their practice from the experiential process, and links the critical incidents to ideas and theories which shed light on them. So, being 'reflective' means exploring experiences (positive and negative, small or large) and moving into new understanding. New understanding is the key feature of a deep approach to learning, as opposed to surface learning or memorising (Marton and Saljo, 1976).

Reflective processes can guide our learning experiences during an event and they can also guide our ability to express or show how this change occurred after the event (Moon, 1999b). Academic assignments might ask you to explore your 'reflections' or thoughts before, during and after an experience. As we have already discussed, 'reflection in action' can be more intuitive and, therefore, harder to articulate later on. Taking the time and space to take a step back from an event, or adopting a 'helicopter view' over it, may help you. Many students have said how reading up on a practice area also helps them clarify their thoughts.

The rule is that reflection for academic purposes usually has to show knowledge, critical thought, analysis, evaluation and output. Deeper levels of reflection will therefore gain more marks than shallow ones, and we will now explore them in detail.

Professional requirements and competences can highlight a number of different aspects and outcomes of reflection as their points of identification. To note an example: in the social work PCF at present, Domain 6 notes the need for reflective practice techniques at ASYE (the first assessed and supported year in employment) level *to evaluate and critically analyse information gained from a variety of sources, to construct and test hypotheses and make explicit evidence-informed decisions.* At an experienced level the need is to *draw on a wide range of evidence sources to inform decision making, to ensure hypotheses and options are reviewed to inform judgement and decision making, and to start to provide professional opinion.* At an advanced level, the need is *to ensure the working environment is maintained where critical reflection and analysis is valued and supported, and routinely provide professional opinion.*

In many instances, because of the rather vague and individual nature of reflection, specific reflective techniques may not be explicitly stated within professional requirements or competences as such, which can leave a practitioner unclear as to what is required. Our next section aims to try and identify particular aspects and levels of the process by examining the common elements within a number of reflective models.

Levels of reflection

There are a number of models of reflection (e.g. Atkins and Murphy, 1994; Johns, 1998; Gibbs, 1998; Driscoll, 2000; Korthagen and Vasalos, 2005; Davys and Beddoe, 2009) that can be followed to develop deeper levels, and your choice will be a personal one. Rolfe et al. (2011) provide a very useful analysis and exploration of the topic. There are certain aspects common to most of these models – a focus on description of an incident, followed by analysis of aims, assumptions, feelings, ethics, behaviours, knowledge, reasoning, decisions, actions and consequences, then an evaluation of the significance of this that leads to learning for future practice. They have been collated and simplified in Table 5.1 in a framework, again with the associated general assessment criteria (QAAHE, 2008).

Table 5.1 Framework of reflective levels with associated assessment criteria

Key levels and aspects of reflection	General assessment criteria
Description Show a full awareness of self and the situation/experience – i.e. What, who, when, where … ?	*Identification, definition*
Critical analysis Identify and explore significant aspects and issues of this situation – e.g. feelings, behaviours, reasoning, decisions, actions, etc. Challenge or question underlying assumptions, knowledge, experience, etc. – i.e. How, why… ?	*Analysis, critical appraisal*
Evaluation Judge input, deliberations, decisions and outcomes; include ideas, information, knowledge, experience, values, professional powers, risk. Show additional insight into relevant issues; wider contexts; different perspectives – i.e. How well … ? What about … ?	*Evaluation, judgement* *Insight, synthesis, creativity*
Learning Produce and evaluate new understandings, perspectives, creative/original solutions, development, change or learning for practice methods and values – i.e. What does this mean …?	*Development of self and practice knowledge* *Personal responsibility* *Professional competences and capabilities*

Of course it is not possible to regard these levels as totally distinct or mutually exclusive from each other and, as seen before, there are many other more implicit elements not included.

ACTIVITY **5.1**

Reflect on one of your own practice experiences using these levels. How does the framework help and hinder this process?

COMMENT

Delving deeper into what was happening can help you uncover the more significant and relevant (but less obvious) aspects that may have been missed or unconsciously passed over. It can also help to understand the part you played and the influence of the wider context too. Sometimes, though, following a series of points on paper misses other more intuitive leaps in our thinking, and it can also become superficial and less critical. Allowing another person to question you should help here.

In our experience, the key barrier to being critically reflexive within reflection is our inability to see how our language, behaviour and responses impact on others. A simple example is when we become irritated by someone else and our tone of voice significantly affects the response of the other person. On reflection later, we could easily forget this feature of the event, or dismiss it as unimportant, preferring to attribute any resulting breakdown in communication to the other person's irritated, angry or unco-operative response. Reflecting with someone else acting as a mentor, supervisor or critical friend can help in this situation as they can help provide a necessary alternative perspective and less biased view of the event or circumstances. If there is a lack of opportunity to reflect with another person, it is an interesting activity to think how you might help someone else to reflect deeply and critically, and then apply the ideas to yourself. The aim is to reflect deeply and critically enough to more fully acknowledge your role in a situation, what was really influencing you and the impact of that on the outcome.

REFLECTION POINT

What additional questions could be, or would need to be, asked at each level in the framework above?

How would you recognise particular barriers to deep reflection that come from a lack of awareness of your role in what occurred, e.g. denial, blinkered views, limited perspective, lack of empathy.

We know that we will, at times, experience strong feelings or inherent beliefs that affect our behaviour and limit our responses to a situation. We need to be able to reflect deeply enough to become aware of these limiting factors in order to be able to address them accordingly. Of course, this is not an easy task but it does lead to more meaningful learning. Korthagen and Vasalos (2005) call it 'core reflection'. Their ALACT model (Action; Looking back on action; Awareness of essential aspects; Creating alternative methods of action; Trial) also provides a structured reflection process, but they combine it with an 'onion model' that deals with the content and underlying issues of that process (from the outer environment and organisation down through levels of behaviour, competences, beliefs and identity towards a central mission). The emphasis here is on identifying and dealing with the limiting factors that prevent achievement of an ideal situation. These could be located on any number of levels within the onion. For example, the authors identify the ways in which a practitioner may be limiting themselves with their behaviour (avoiding confrontation), feelings (of powerless) and beliefs (that this is something I have no influence over). By formulating the ideal situation, together with the factors experienced as inhibiting the achievement of that ideal, the person becomes aware of an *inner tension or discrepancy*. The point is that once the limiting factors are recognised we have a choice over whether or not to allow them to determine our behaviour – if we reflect in this way, we can start to ask some fundamental questions with regard to such choices. The authors also identify a need for core qualities or character strengths to become mobilised in response here, e.g. creativity, courage, kindness, fairness. Their examples focus on a teaching environment, but again, the essential features relate on a human level to all of us.

Core reflection like this will, therefore, challenge deep and personally held beliefs, assumptions or inner values. When this happens you will need the extra support of someone you trust to help you deal with it, so it is important you recognise this as soon as it starts to happen. The need for safe and facilitated/supported learning environments therefore becomes essential to help actualise such qualities and enable an awareness of new possibilities for action.

Can it end up a bit negative?

It can feel negative when things we try in practice don't turn out the way we expect. We can start to feel anxious and defensive when having to think about it all again. But we are dealing with real life and your supervisor or tutors will actually expect a conflict between prior expectations and experiences – as we have seen, this is how deep learning can occur. What is required is that this conflict is not ignored or glossed over but explored further with kindness in order to develop practice. 'False accounts' of reflection can be fairly easy to spot. If you are at all unsure about how much or what you are supposed to 'reveal', ask your tutors to be as explicit as possible regarding what they are looking for. They should distinguish between what is deemed 'public information', and thus used for assessment, and what is personal and private.

Understanding new ideas can involve the reassessment of old perspectives, which can be discomforting, whereas exploring the things that have gone right can affirm and help understanding of experience and knowledge in more detail. But reflecting on all types of experiences (the negative and positive) can:

- allow greater awareness and expression of all types of learning and development;
- show enhanced understanding about why things did work, as well as why they didn't;
- provide a more positive ending for the negative experiences rather than just leaving things as they were, and allow a proper and full recognition of the good experiences and one's strengths.

We also need to understand how to apply or transfer these strengths and work with them in new or more difficult situations. We already possess much of what we need to develop but a lot of it lies hidden or unrecognised unless it is reflected on. Reflection on problems can weaken confidence to develop in self-reflective ways (Weick et al., 1989) but a shift towards possibilities creates new, positive and individual paths for people. This is a 'strengths-perspective' approach for enabling others. Learning to transfer strengths from one setting to another is a key component in lifelong learning.

However, placing oneself at the centre of an event or experience can lead to a preoccupation with the self that can border on self-absorption. To avoid this happening, ensure that your reflection turns outwards as well, i.e. on to practice values, principles, traditions and the wider organisational or social context relevant to the issue. Also be aware that reflection is not foolproof. Remembering the past is dependent on many different factors and is fallible. Early work by Newell (1992) notes the range of ways reflection is inherently flawed, relating it to the inaccurate, biased and selective way we initially process information and then recall it. The fallibility of our memory means that the event or action as recalled is probably not what really happened in its entirety, and so the value of any reflection upon it has to be questioned at a fundamental level. When reflecting back on an experience the original event becomes shaped and coloured by that reflective action too, especially if the event was stressful and the practitioner sees a need to protect themselves. Many courses advise the keeping of notes or a journal of some sort to record and preserve what actually happened in detail and enable more accurate recall at a later date. Newell (1992) also suggests checklists or group discussions to aid memory, the help of a mentor, quick debriefing sessions and/or use of anxiety management or stress-reduction techniques within the reflective process.

Other useful activities to develop reflection are questioning and sharing thoughts with others, which is why group work and communication with colleagues and fellow students is particularly important for most CPD situations.

Review

Reflecting deeply and critically is about making sure that all the aspects above are covered, i.e. there is an evaluated outcome or conclusion in terms of your understanding and learning and development. These ideas provide the necessary elements to write about for CPD learning, but it is important to understand academic writing style in order to articulate ideas in the correct way when in a formal learning environment. The following chapter will elaborate on this.

FURTHER READING

Knott, C and Scragg, T (2013) *Reflective practice in social work.* 3rd edition. London: Sage/Learning Matters.

An introductory text that explores a range of approaches and ideas associated with reflective practice.

Rolfe, G, Freshwater, D and Jasper, M (2011) *Critical reflection in practice: Generating knowledge for care.* 2nd edition. London: Palgrave Macmillan.

This practical user's guide offers a range of clear frameworks and structures of reflective practice, including individual and group supervision, reflective writing and research.

Taylor, C and White, S (2000) *Practising reflexivity in health and welfare: Making knowledge.* Buckingham: Open University Press.

This book explores how knowledge is used in professional practice and how it is constructed in everyday encounters.

Thompson, S and Thompson, N (2008) *The critically reflective practitioner.* London: Palgrave Macmillan.

This is essential reading for making sense of reflective practice, looking at what it is, what it is not and what it can be at its best.

Chapter 6
Writing reflective academic assignments

This section focuses on reflective academic assignments in the first person which aim to integrate theory and practice and articulate professional judgement. It suggests ways to structure and write them using the guidelines we give our own students. This guidance is based on years of teaching experience and of external assessment, so we feel confident of its value, but not all universities adopt this style of assignment. Different institutions will assess reflective assignments in various ways for each of the academic levels, so it is necessary to check with your tutors before you follow the guidance given here. How you view any assignment will depend on your previous experiences of education and the length of time since being a formal 'learner', but it will be important not to make any assumptions and obviously to follow your course handbooks and assignment guidelines very carefully.

In general, the reflective assignment needs to evidence the understanding and use of academic knowledge, the learning outcomes achieved and professional development. It is therefore not a description of events or feelings. It should allow the learning derived from your critical thinking and reflection to be expressed.

Benefits of writing

Academic assessment can be dominated by written work. As with most qualifications it is not what you think or do, but the way you articulate it that is graded. Assignment writing is therefore important because it is a major way in which existing or developing practice can be expressed for assessment purposes. This is a positive aspect because we understand and learn more while we are writing because the process supports and develops reflective and critical abilities. It is also a skill all health and social workers must acquire as it is often via written reports that clients are represented.

According to Moon (1999a), writing:

- forces us to spend the time;
- helps us focus and sift material by slowing us down;
- forces us to organise and clarify our thoughts so we can sequence them;
- gives us a structure;

- gives control – we choose which points to make – which enables identification and prioritising of material;
- helps us to know if we do understand something by attempting to explain it;
- can help develop a deeper understanding of something as we work through it and explain it;
- can record a train of thought and relate it to the past, present and future;
- can initiate new ideas, connections, questions, etc.

Because critical reflection relies so much on making connections and judging thoughts and information, writing is one of the main activities that can help by starting this process of capturing and expressing basic assumptions, underlying knowledge and the memory of any experience. Writing skills are primarily thinking skills but because writing is slower it can achieve more, especially in developing connections between ideas, exploring the experience more deeply and gaining different perspectives.

Writing is not a one-off activity. All writing is about drafting and rewriting. It has a powerful effect in prompting further insights and hunches – the problem is that once we write these down they sound clumsy. This is because these ideas come into our minds as holistic and compacted 'nuggets', if you like. To convey them in structured language is like trying to translate them from one code into another. It won't happen in one or two attempts, unfortunately. Also, this translation process will throw up further ideas as we explore and unravel the original one. It is no wonder we go off on tangents and get lost. The key is to have a structure and a disciplined approach so that we can work with and control these thoughts and articulate a clear message from them.

Coverage

Choosing what to write about will obviously depend entirely on what the assignment is for, but it will usually be concerned with new knowledge becoming embedded in practice. A study of the assignment content guidelines and intended learning outcomes will identify the main areas to cover. List these main areas and develop some ideas around them, then decide which experiences or examples will be able to show and evidence these areas best, or plan for a new experience to allow this. How you do this is up to you; everyone has a different way, whether it's using lists or pictures. But do start – even if it's with 'Once a upon a time … '. Only when something is down on paper or on a computer screen can you begin to work on it and make it better – if it's stuck in your head it's probably just going to float about doing nothing except worry you.

Using the reflective levels

As we have seen, reflecting in a CPD context is about concentrating on the deeper, critical levels to ensure that there is an outcome in terms of your understanding, evaluation and learning about the education and practice events you are involved with – your professional development. If we re-examine the reflective levels, we can see that the questions associated with each of them can also help develop our initial, often more descriptive, thoughts and reflections on to more analytical and evaluative levels. See Table 6.1.

Table 6.1 Questions to develop descriptive reflection towards learning

Description	Critical analysis	Evaluation	Learning
What did you do? What happened? What did you feel?	How did you do it? Why did you do it that way and not a different way? What was important and significant – why?	How far and in what ways were your goals met? What other factors were apparent?	So what does this mean for future practice and your values?

We can go further and identify the type of material that might need to be included in answers to these questions at each level. See Table 6.2.

Table 6.2 Type of material to include at each reflective level

Description	Critical analysis	Evaluation	Learning
Background	Theory, research, policy, legislation	Judgement, measurement of progress and outcome/s	Abstracting general principles
Context	Experience, practice knowledge	Strengths, weaknesses, gaps	Insights, ideas, new perspectives
Feelings	Values, ethics, conflicts	Counter-arguments and theories	Synthesis with existing knowledge
Specific relevant details	Aims and objectives	Wider context, other factors	Professional development
Definitions	Judgements, assumptions	Different perspectives	Future planning, changes
	Decisions, deliberations; reflection 'before, in and after action'	Alternatives	Further theory, research

Table 6.2 mainly follows a 'reflection-on-action' idea (Schön, 1983) and a linear progression from left to right. It is not meant to be a prescriptive approach and you can use it in any way that helps. However, there is much this table cannot account for, i.e. the subtlety, depth, emotion and intuition involved in learning and thinking. Some of the questions or areas may not be relevant to your experience or reflection, and your own individual style and approach may require more holistic guidance to follow.

We are merely suggesting that reflective writing is a developmental and ongoing process, requiring time and feedback, and the elements noted above are all-important aspects to be included because they are the elements usually being assessed. At its heart, CPD learning is about the demonstration of competence and capability to practise and this cannot occur without reflection on your practice.

Structure: developing an 'argument'

Stage 1: developing a viewpoint and starting to make an argument

The starting point for structuring an assignment of this type is your overall point of view, your central idea or your basic 'claim'. You cannot really start writing a first complete draft until you know what it is you want to say. And you won't know this until all the stages of the reflection process, and initial reading of the subject area, have been achieved. Your viewpoint consists of what has been understood and learnt, plus what this means for your practice and values. A viewpoint forms the basis of your overall 'argument' and allows you to control the material and develop your own voice. This does not mean that the assignment has to formally argue for or against something. It simply means that there has to be a coherent thread or series of connected points running through it that reach a conclusion, pursuing an idea and/or the implications of an issue in practice. If you get stuck at this stage use Table 6.1, which may help you to reflect more deeply. If you still feel lost, try discussing with a tutor or supervisor. Even the smallest practice incidents can be packed with implicit new knowledge or learning, but you may not be able to see it for yourself without some critical questioning.

Developing the confidence to work with material in a way that allows your unique interpretation to be valued is a key underpinning aspect of CPD learning. As we have seen, recent literature concerning professional knowledge in health and social work emphasises the legitimate generation of practice-based knowledge, where practice expertise is integrated with formal knowledge, and which is able to take full account of the complexity and uncertainty of practice (e.g. Fook et al., 2000; Mathews and Crawford, 2011).

The following is a simplified example of a viewpoint.

Example

Assignment: enabling a student on placement

Stage 1: my viewpoint or the central idea

'Good communication seems to be essential when planning successfully for a placement student.'

Notes – I have learnt that because we need people in order to achieve things, communicating effectively with them helps us achieve more. This is another way we can show respect to others. The literature on placement planning generally agrees. Some authors do not give this area a lot of emphasis, though.

Stage 2: reasons give the structure a sequence

Once your viewpoint is known, you can then focus any further reflection and research on the pivotal themes and issues that form and establish this point of view, i.e. the reasons that support it. These can consist of formal and informal knowledge and evidence at this stage. For a 5,000-word assignment you will probably only be able to focus effectively on three or four main reasons. These reasons should be organised in a way that can best persuade your reader to agree. Too often we pick a subject that is just too big. Focus down – this will give you space to be analytical.

By expressing your viewpoint and reasons/themes in this way, you are making a claim, and the next stage is to sustain this claim in response to (or in anticipation of) a 'challenge' when you are in an academic environment. In other words, you now have to show the validity of this view and your commitment to it. This is not unusual, unique or inappropriate – health and social workers are constantly justifying their decisions and actions when challenged by service users, managers or colleagues in practice.

We can refer back to our viewpoint example and show some reasons for it.

Example
Assignment for a specialist area of social work: enabling others

Stage 1: my viewpoint

'Good communication seems to be essential when planning successfully for a placement student.'

Stage 2: the reasons why I believe good communication is essential

1. Interpersonal skills (good listening) helped me start the relationship with the student well – empathy, trust being built. Literature on interpersonal communication says these skills are crucial in forming relationships and for education. Dangers to be aware of are becoming too informal and friendly ...

2. Better forming of communication lines with the university tutor would have enabled better understanding of their role and the ways I needed to liaise with them. I felt intimidated, and assumed the tutor would not be available; bureaucracy issues were apparent. Literature on placements says this is a difficult area – need to be proactive. I can discuss ways I could do this better next time ...

3. Liaison with my team beforehand helped the induction go smoothly – people on side, better prepared. Literature about team co-ordination says that early contact allows problems to surface and be dealt with before we start. Literature on placement planning says early contact is essential but to also keep overall control by forming clear learning objectives for the student.

ACTIVITY **6.1**

If such a structure is useful to you, start to develop one for an assignment of your own. Our example was very linear in structure but you can do it using any method you like.

COMMENT

Understanding and deciding what your main viewpoint is may take some time and may also change as you start writing and/or read more material. This is usual as it is a learning process, but it means you need to continue to reflect and also focus. Revisit any assignment guidance and intended learning outcomes to make sure you are covering relevant topics etc. and not going off-track.

Stage 3: developing points for each reason will make up the paragraphs

Under each of your reasons develop a series of smaller but key points, using paragraphs, to show how and why they are relevant etc., using evidence from theory/research/ policy/legislation/experience/values to discuss/debate/challenge ideas presented. Each reason or theme will then need its own 'conclusion' which links back to the main argument/point of view.

By showing where evidence has come from (by citing and referencing it), or showing how it has been formed as a robust process, you can demonstrate its authority, reliability and validity for this purpose; in other words, apply relevant critical standards to it. Also look for material that contradicts your opinions to show that you are aware of, and have considered, arguments that are counter to your own. This will help clarify and sharpen your own ideas and help you demonstrate why they are more convincing. Their use is a good guiding critical principle. We have already shown in Chapter 4 how you can use the literature in practice more directly by critically examining how and why you adapted an idea for your own use, i.e. evaluate its purpose and usefulness for a situation.

To achieve an appropriate academic style you must view all knowledge as contextual (Baxter Magolda, 1992), i.e. there are no completely right or wrong answers out there, but the knowledge or evidence supporting opinions and views can be constructed, understood and appraised in relation to a particular context or situation. As we have said, there is no absolute 'truth' and your tutor will be assessing your ability to gain an overview of the subject and support a particular position in relation to your practice situation within it.

Paragraphs and signposting

Remember the idea is to try to persuade the reader. Often the first sentence is the key point itself, i.e. it explains what the paragraph is about and contains the main idea.

This 'topic sentence' need not come first in the paragraph, but it has to be somewhere because it asserts and controls the paragraph's main idea. You can place it in the middle if you have information that needs to precede it. You can put it at the end if you want your reader to consider your line of reasoning before you declare your main point.

A topic sentence is important because it helps organise a paragraph by summarising the information in it. It lets the reader know what the paragraph is about and so the sentences that follow it have to give more information about that sentence, e.g. by explaining further or providing evidence for it. (This sounds obvious but very often we can go off on a tangent and miss the main point altogether!) Every topic sentence will have a topic and a controlling idea. The controlling idea shows the content of the paragraph and the direction it will take.

Here are some examples:

1. Topic sentence: *Dogs make wonderful pets because they can help you live longer.* The topic is 'dogs make wonderful pets' and the controlling idea is 'because they can help you live longer'. So the paragraph will explore a number of ways dogs help you live longer (e.g. by reducing stress), using evidence as required to support but also challenge the ideas, and show why this makes them wonderful pets.

2. Topic sentence: *There are many reasons why infection control in Trust X is the best in the country.* The topic is 'infection control in Trust X is the best in the country' and the controlling idea is 'many reasons'. So the paragraph will explore the reasons in turn to explain why infection control is the best, but also critically challenge them and/or discuss any other evidence which refutes this.

3. Topic sentence: *To be an effective leader requires certain characteristics.* The topic is 'to be an effective leader' and the controlling idea is 'certain characteristics'. So the paragraph will explore the characteristics that various models suggest effective leaders require (and therefore help explore what 'effective' means), allowing the discussion to explore the 'why' and 'how' of each, plus allow a critical view on the credibility or authority of any model, and make a conclusion overall.

4. Topic sentence: *Teenage pregnancy may be prevented by improved education.* The topic is 'teenage pregnancy may be prevented' and the controlling idea is 'improving education'. So the paragraph will provide a nuanced and critical view of both issues and explore the connections between them in order to demonstrate the ways in which education may be improved to prevent teenage pregnancy.

As you can see, the *topic sentence* provides the essential focus for the reader; it tells us what the paragraph is about and makes a point. The *controlling idea* provides the sub-areas you then expand on – there may be a list of items, e.g. in (2) the reasons will be explored in turn and in (3) the characteristics will be explored; or an area may be opened up further, e.g. in (1) exactly how dogs help you live longer would be explored further, in (3) the notion of effectiveness can be examined, and in (4) the ways teenage pregnancy can be perceived, what 'improved' education means and any connections between them would be explored. So the controlling idea helps the reader understand what you are saying by explaining and exploring the issue further, usually with the literature and/or practice examples. Using this system with the other advice in this section really helps to stop you going off at a tangent.

However you do it, the line of reasoning and its evidence should be linked logically within these paragraphs. As you develop the point you tell the reader where you are going with it, by making use of the literature, linking back to the reason and the main argument as appropriate. Ideally, it is best to sort out one point before moving on to another, but if you do need to stop and then return to a point later, make sure you tell the reader what you are doing and why.

The next point should always be introduced. Using linking words or 'signposts' helps the reader make the transition from one paragraph or point to the next. There are different ways to do this depending on the way you want to develop your argument.

Here are some examples.

- Contrast, or taking a sudden turn in reasoning – 'but ...', 'however ...', 'on the other hand ...', 'although ...', 'and yet ...'

- Cause and effect – 'therefore ...', 'as a result of ...', 'for this reason ...', 'consequently ...'

- Sequence – 'following ... ', 'before ...', 'first ...', finally ...'

- Illustration – 'for example ...', 'for instance ...', 'such as ...', 'in this case ...'

- Add weight – 'similarly ...', 'in addition ...', 'moreover ...'

- Conclusion – 'in conclusion ...', 'accordingly ...', 'to sum up ...'

Returning to our example we can see a specific point being developed for the first reason.

Example
Assignment for a specialist area of social work: enabling others

Stage 1: my viewpoint

'Good communication seems to be essential when planning successfully for a placement student.'

Stage 2: first reason

1. 'Interpersonal skills (good listening) helped me start the relationship with the student well – empathy, trust being built.'

(Continued)

(Continued)

Stage 3: particular point/issue to develop for this reason

This is the point (topic sentence) – Listening to the student rather than talking at her made our initial meeting a very positive one.

Define – 'Listening entails ...'

Develop – how and why – 'Letting the student speak first not only allowed me an understanding of her unique situation and needs, it also made her feel at ease with me and to start to trust me ...'

Link to reason/argument – 'Understanding her needs and circumstances informed my planning ...; but this conversation also formed a bond between us ...'

Evidence/connections – 'Bloggs (2003) explains how listening is more important than talking because it shows respect to others ... and she responded by ...' 'Adult learning theory similarly emphasises the need for respect for learners ...'

Link to next point/paragraph – 'However, the relationship still needs to remain professional ...'

Once your main text is structured you will need an introduction and a conclusion.

Introduction

We want to emphasise the crucial importance of the introduction. This is probably the most important part of your work in terms of ensuring your writing keeps to task. Don't attempt it until you have a good grip on your argument, reasons and points.

- Set the overall context and also state the main viewpoint and the issues you are going to write about and why. It will help you focus and place your 'argument' into a wider picture.

- Point out the limitations and what you are not going to consider.

Introduce the structure and sequence of your work.

Conclusion

A conclusion is all too often just a paragraph stuck on the end of the piece of work, which either summarises what has come before or gives the result of what happened.

A conclusion offers the chance to do much more than this. It can deliver a concise consideration of the overall meaning you have gained from critical thinking and reflection on your practice and/or learning. That is, it can sum up the major issues and points raised from your evaluation of the outcomes and consequences, plus what they may or will mean for social work, for your practice or for yourself.

ACTIVITY **6.2**

Try writing a brief introduction for our example assignment.

COMMENT

It is useful if the introduction provides some linking phrases to tell the reader where you are going (or what you have shown) with your ideas. For example, an introduction could say: This assignment will look initially at … to show that … ; followed by an examination of … to demonstrate that …; while exploring issues around … to understand how …

Critical style

Developing an appropriate critical style does take time and practice, especially when initial thoughts tend to be very descriptive – here are some more tips. Table 6.3 shows how the more normal, descriptive way of writing can be developed into a critical academic style by listing how each element should be enhanced. Again, we can see similar methods of questioning, delving deeper, assessing and judging things as we do in critical thinking abilities.

Table 6.3 Descriptive to critical writing (Cottrell, 2003, p232)

Descriptive writing	Critical analytical writing
States what happened	Identifies the significance
States what something is like	Evaluates (judges the value of) strengths and weaknesses
Gives the story so far	Weighs one piece of information against another
States the order in which things happened	Makes reasoned judgements
Says how to do something	Argues a case according to the evidence
Explains what a theory says	Shows why something is relevant or suitable
Explains how something works	Indicates why something will work (best)
Notes the method used	Indicates whether something is appropriate or suitable
Says when something occurred	Identifies why the timing is of importance
States the different components	Weighs up the importance of component parts
States options	Gives reasons for selecting each option
Lists details	Evaluates the relative significance of details
Lists in any order	Structures information in order of importance
States links between items	Shows the relevance of links between pieces of info
Gives information	Draws conclusions

Academic style: some hints for vocabulary and grammar

Try more formal, specific words, e.g.:

- 'examine' instead of 'look at';

- 'has the potential' instead of 'might';

- 'enables' instead of 'makes it possible'.

Try the passive voice in places.

- 'Assessments are started by gathering relevant information' instead of 'You start assessments by gathering relevant information'.

Use more cautious language to avoid sweeping statements.

- 'The introduction of the new policy could be seen as ...'

Use noun phrases which cut down the use of words, especially verbs for a more succinct text.

- 'Carer's rights' instead of 'The rights of the carer'.

- 'Recently issued policies' instead of 'Policies that have been issued recently'.

- 'The effectiveness of the treatments made them very popular' instead of 'The treatments were effective and this made them very popular'.

Using the literature

As you probably realise, your success very much depends on the type of literature you read (its relevancy and authority) and your understanding of it, not how much you read. Quality not quantity! As a practitioner you will also be using contextual information such as legislation, case law, policy and practice guidance documents, as well as theory and research. Your tutor, your reading lists and handouts will direct you to relevant and authoritative literature, and you will be looking up more references for any specialist areas, using print and electronic resources. The particular problem areas associated with using literature are detailed below.

Making unsubstantiated comments

One of the biggest single pieces of advice given back to students is 'Do not make unsubstantiated comments, or sweeping generalisations'. Be clear about the difference between making points regarding your own practice and about social work practice in general. Evidence from your own practice experiences should be discussed as evaluated reflective practice rather than as mere anecdotes. Formal knowledge will help critically discuss the points you are making, but it is important to know how far it is expected to 'back you up' and whether you are allowed to discuss your expertise in a way that also evidences its own authority rather than relying entirely on the authority of others.

Any generalised assertions, ideas and opinions made about your profession in a broader sense, though, do require evidence from external, formal sources (in the form of references to previous writers, policies, legislation, etc.) to firmly support them.

We believe that in order to effectively develop their expertise, post-qualifying learners in particular should not be expected to rely entirely on the ideas or authority of others in relation to their practice. They need to be able to discuss their development of practice and practice-based knowledge in a way that evidences its own authority, e.g. via sound practical reasoning, judgement or decision-making, as well as using formal knowledge to help critically inform, explain or explore the points being made.

Avoiding plagiarism

You need to say where any evidence or ideas which are not your own have come from, otherwise you will be making claims to research/ideas/etc. that are not yours (which is plagiarism). Therefore references to evidence in the literature should appear whenever you are mentioning another's ideas, theory, material or research, whether you are directly quoting or paraphrasing them. This has to follow certain academic 'rules' in order to be valid and you should follow the appropriate system as advocated by your academic institution.

You can use someone else's work in three main ways (the following references are for illustration only):

1. You can mention their theory or idea:

   The process used incorporated some of the elements of task-centred work (Marsh and Doel, 2005) and systems approach (Milner and O'Byrne, 1998; Walker, 2012) because the ...

2. You can summarise in your own words what someone else has written, either small sections or overall views:

   Mrs Jones felt helpless and frustrated at her inability to improve her daughter's situation and appeared to get many colds and coughs during this time, which weakened her ability to look after her. Research has shown that those who experience life events that are seen as uncontrollable are more likely to become ill (Stern et al., 2003, cited in Gross, 2004).

3. You can repeat a small section of what someone has written and place it in quotation marks, or indent it:

   It is not sufficient to be reflective; we also need to use new understandings in our future actions. As Adams et al. (2002, p87) point out: 'reflection on its own views the situation unchanged, whereas critical practice is capable of change'.

When paraphrasing:

- express the person's main ideas in your own words;
- keep it simple and concise;
- don't use the same sentence structure.

Try this method of remembering how to present other people's evidence: Ask – 'says who?' and 'so what?' In other words, say who says this – the idea and the reference to who said it, and then state why you are telling the reader this – what is your point here? Often we read assignments and case studies and ask ourselves what is the point of the writer telling us that because it just appears to be packaging. Always ask yourself: 'what am I trying to say and why is it important?' It will help you to be more focused.

If you use quotes, 'pick out' the key words and extend the discussion with them and the ideas being presented, e.g.:

> Smith (2012, p55) advocates that, 'it is very important that everyone involved in a process of improving service quality has a shared understanding of the issues and what is expected of them'. Sharing and understanding expectations are therefore key aspects to bear in mind when communicating with colleagues ... however ...

Or paraphrase, and then lead into the discussion and start to support the point being made:

> It is essential that expectations are shared and understood by everyone involved in situations concerning service improvement (Smith, 2012). Communication strategies are therefore of major importance ... however ...

or:

> A key aim with service quality development is clear communication and an exchange of information and ideas for staff, especially about roles and the type of activities they would be involved with. As Smith (2012) shows, it is essential that expectations are shared and understood in such situations. However ...

Whichever way you use the work of other people, you must cite where the work came from in the text itself and provide a reference to the complete work in either a references list or a bibliography at the end of your work. In the Harvard system of referencing, the citation in the text uses the author's last name and year, and the references list or bibliography will be in alphabetical order by author's last name. It is important to look up the referencing rules for your particular institution and become familiar with them.

Effective reading

It does take time and practice to develop your reading in order to locate relevant and useful material. Here are a few initial ideas to help you start.

- Use any guidance provided by an educational institution or training department on gaining access to and using the most relevant electronic databases and printed materials. Use librarians for advice too. You don't want to waste time at this end of the process.

- Reading the literature while you are developing your viewpoint should encompass the wider topic area. Reading when you know what your viewpoint is will enable you to focus and identify the more relevant pieces of text easily and save your time. Make a note of particular quotes (keep them as short as possible) or paraphrase ideas (summarise in your own words). Also note the complete reference to the book, journal etc. at the time.

- Next, write down a brief explanation of what this means to you: what do you understand it to mean – do you agree or disagree with it – why? This becomes easier if you are applying what you read into practice straight away, or you have opportunities for discussion about the literature with your peers.

- As we have seen, as you start writing the first draft of your assignment you will have a good idea of what you are trying to say, so when you refer back to these notes you can choose those that are applicable to what you are talking about and integrate them.

Using the first person 'I'

N.B. You must check your institution's own rules on this – some universities do not allow the use of the first person in written assignments.

Using the first-person 'I' is appropriate for academic reflective writing and for developing personal and professional qualities of self-awareness, reflection, analysis and critique (Hamill, 1999). However, this does not mean the writing should be emotional or subjective, i.e. seen from your viewpoint only. Students who lack experience in writing and who start to use 'I' tend to be too descriptive in their style, e.g. 'I did this ...' 'I did that ...'. So 'I' has to be used carefully and much care has to be taken to avoid informal or conversational tones within a reflective assignment. Using 'I' should encourage a confident stance, i.e. directness in saying what you mean and the message you are trying to get across. With the addition of the literature, and your viewpoint and reasons, it creates an appropriate academic style.

Finishing writing

Check coverage and relevancy – match what you say you will focus on in the introduction against what you have written about in the main body and the conclusion. Also, refer back to your original list of what the assignment has to cover – make sure you have covered all that is asked of you. Ask yourself – 'where have I shown this?'

Think critically about your work before handing it in. Evaluate it using the guidance given here or even try marking it using your institution's assessment criteria.

Review

As we have seen, writing is a process. Each draft will enable you to show areas of learning and development in more structured, explicit and academic ways as you build up a better understanding of what you have done. The main difficulty with writing is to get the real meaning of what you are trying to say past the code of language in which you have to say it.

Each rewrite should allow this by giving you the opportunity to:

- think about and analyse what you want to say more thoroughly;

- reflect on what you have achieved or learnt more deeply;

- read more around the issues and increase your ability to express your understanding of the links to the literature.

By enabling a clear and deeper understanding of learning and practice development, the processes of writing should enhance critical practice, which is itself a process of self-enquiry and, at times, transformative change. Our next chapter looks at these ideas more closely.

FURTHER READING

Cottrell, S (2013) *The study skills handbook.* 4th edition. London: Palgrave Macmillan.

A handy reference guide to thinking, learning, research, reading and writing skills for academic study.

Foote, S, Quinney, A and Taylor, M (2103) *The social work assignments handbook.* Harlow: Pearson.

Useful for undergraduate and postgraduate social work students, giving guidance and examples for assignment and projects.

Watson, F, Burrows, H and Player, C (2002) *Integrating theory and practice in social work education.* London: Jessica Kingsley.

A clear and instructive text gives practical advice on how to write better essays or assessments and give better presentations within social work, although it is aimed at diploma-level study only.

Chapter 7
Developing critical practice

Our aim in this chapter is to develop some of the topics and ideas seen in previous chapters while focusing on more critical approaches to practice rather than particular methods and techniques. Every day health and social work practitioners deal with risk, complexity and uncertainty, and so:

- there will be range of 'solutions';

- things will change;

- outcomes cannot be predicted with utter certainty;

- certain values and assumptions may not be valid in the future;

- there will be many other perspectives on a situation.

Working with the stress and vagaries of such practice, by allowing for contingency and checking up on how things are going, is more likely to lessen its threat and its ability to make us feel defensive. We need practices that allow us to accept and deal with ever-changing situations creatively, rather than practices that only make us follow prescriptions. As we have established, it is useful to consider critical thinking for practice within its widest and most holistic sense as 'being critical' or 'taking a critical stance', and this involves a practitioner's overall approach to their work.

To do this we will continue to explore how practitioners develop their expertise and professional judgement, but also gain the understandings and open mindset necessary to approach the uncertainty of practice in a positive way. We then look pragmatically at where criticality fits within these ways of working.

First, we can examine how practice is developed over time. Many of these ideas are based on Fook et al.'s (2000) research on the development of expertise.

New practice

Once qualified, or indeed when taking up any new post or starting a placement, a practitioner's professional development and learning start to focus on a range of work-related aspects and knowledge.

The most obvious relates to a particular workplace setting or activity system and is bound up with the systems' rules, tools, norms, objectives, divisions of labour and communities of practice.

(Knight et al., 2006, p32)

Beginning to deal with this type of 'how to' knowledge is where a new practitioner's lack of experience becomes obvious and can cause anxiety due to a resulting lack of confidence. As seen earlier, it may well be the reason why many newly qualified workers take a very prescriptive, rule-based approach to try to ensure they do not do anything wrong. However, such a focus on detail and correctness can also ensure that new practitioners will be more critically aware of what they are doing than the more experienced workers who have established 'uncritical' routines.

The key for workers in these situations is to attain a balance between the need for certainty and the need to be aware of other ways of doing, or thinking about, practice. Here is where critical reflection (especially involving others) can play a key role in developing confidence through the analysis of strengths-based practice, but also allow consideration of alternative options, viewpoints, etc., within a safe space, and ensure that a blinkered and uncritical rigidity does not get established.

Good critical thinking should evolve alongside a person's development within their practice. However, there is an important issue to take account of. The aim of many critical methods is to create doubt and critique of ongoing actions but it is difficult to act confidently and thoughtfully while doubting oneself at the same time (Van Manen, 1995). We can, however, adopt critical practice more as an acceptable way of 'being' by undertaking tasks in positive and confident, but also open and flexible ways. To achieve this it is necessary to embed criticality as an approach within professional and experienced practice itself, rather than use critical methods as remedial 'bolt-ons', which are more likely to suffer when workloads rise.

We look first at the dangers of developing in practice uncritically.

The dangers of more experience

On a day-to-day level there are dangers associated with the development of expertise in practice. Any practice can easily fall into purely intuitive and routine methods that are followed because they are safer and less time-consuming. We develop rules of thumb and standardise our approaches to problems in order to survive our workloads. However, these habitual practices are more difficult to keep under critical control and they tend not to adapt to new circumstances easily.

In these situations uncertain problems may be 'pretended' to be certain so we can accommodate them into existing practices or our value systems, or they are simplified by ignoring certain difficult aspects. Matching similarities is easier than acknowledging dissimilarities because they confirm rather than deny our generalisations and so fit our existing knowledge. As human beings we tend to give more credence to viewpoints that are close to our own, and tend to devalue or reject information that conflicts with our beliefs. This saves time and energy and makes us feel less threatened because knowledge relies for its verification on belief, but eventually the process of evaluating our work becomes lost.

As we become less subject to dissimilarity and surprise, our experiences become non-learning situations, as we don't notice what is actually happening. So even though we have more experience in a particular environment we do not automatically acquire more valid knowledge.

In this respect, the main benefits that our students report when undertaking our programmes are that they:

- provide reassurance of good practices already being undertaken via discussion with others and use of the literature; but they also

- enable them to stop, think and reassess their practice, which allows them to see where they have fallen into pure routine and adopt more appropriate methods and approaches.

Learning new knowledge, talking to others, sharing ideas, applying and connecting them to practice and then reflecting on what happens, engages the brain in a different mode. Post-qualifying and other CPD programmes can encourage better quality approaches through their content and assessment, plus allow the opportunity and encouragement to undertake more critical work practices.

REFLECTION POINT

Which areas of your own practice have become habitual and routine?

Embedding criticality

If we look at a more positive model of expertise we can see how the holistic notion of professionally developed practice requires a critical overall disposition or stance, and also where critical thinking can be embedded as an approach to enhance existing practice.

Research adapted from Cust (1995, cited in Macaulay, 2000) shows how experienced practitioners (or 'experts' as they call them) encounter new situations.

They:

- are in control of their thinking, i.e. aware of, understand, self-direct and self-evaluate it throughout;

- have clusters of 'tacit knowledge' which form 'patterns' and represent the learning and generalising from previous experiences, from research and theory;

- recognise other meaningful patterns and principles, and irrelevant aspects, in a situation and link to these existing known patterns;

- o and so gain an intuitive grasp of the situation;

- o while assessing it in depth;

- o in order to select 'schemas' (patterns or outlines formed in the mind);

- o which, when adapted to the problem, are likely to effectively represent it as well as suggesting solution procedures;

- o but will periodically check to review, progress and evaluate outcomes.

Such 'experts' are seen to focus initially on the holistic assessment of a situation, rather than on explicit reasoning and analysis. In other words, they have established the necessary intuitive links to bring the different parts of a situation into a meaningful whole, to allow it to make sense for them. Each situation they face may be different but they will recognise enough of the parts to make general sense of the whole, in order to start to deal with it. Schön (1983) explained this by stating that experienced practitioners know how to define the nature of the problem or situation first – they can more easily 'name and frame' a situation.

Embedding critical thinking and developing holistic critical approaches

If we now list the key expert practice areas gathered from the ideas above we can begin to see where relevant critical thinking activities can be most appropriately and positively embedded. As we can see in Table 7.1, our earlier ideas associated with professional judgement and practical reasoning are pertinent here and have been incorporated as well.

Table 7.1 Elements and activities of critical 'expert' practice

'Expert' practice areas	Embedded critical thinking
1. Awareness, control and evaluation of thinking processes	Thinking about thinking (meta-thinking). Recognising and questioning arguments, etc. Identifying and challenging own and others' assumptions.
2. Developing clusters of knowledge	Keeping up to date; reading the literature. Integrating values and experience. Holding views based on valid experiential evidence but seeking and accepting relevant but alternative viewpoints and perspectives. Generating and evaluating practice-based knowledge.
3. Assessment of situations in depth – 'naming and framing' Selection and adaptation of 'schema' or framework that fits	Gaining alternative perspective/s or reframing a situation. Understanding when more information and input is required, knowing where and how to get it. Lateral/creative/flexible thinking; problem forming and solving.
4. Decisions leading to action	Decision-making and planning; use of discretion; responsibility; risk assessment.

	Seeking out and taking proper account of all stakeholders' input. Thinking through the means–end relationship as well as the implications of decisions and actions.
	Predicting possible outcomes, allowing for alternatives.
5. *Monitoring progress and evaluating outcomes. Adapting and changing where necessary. Ongoing learning*	Formulating clear aims/objectives at the start, getting feedback and making judgements.
	Using feedback and evaluation from all concerned parties, especially people who use services.
	Making informal leaning more explicit. Embedding formal learning.
	Sharing and developing learning within the organisation.

As we can see, there are many critical thinking activities that can be aligned and embedded within areas of expert practice to allow the best possible (i.e. most critical) approaches. However, it is not just about 'bolting on' a set of separate standards, strategies or methods to existing practice (although these may be important at various points). As seen throughout this text, the notion of true critical practice becomes established with inherent approaches to various work practices and with holistic habits of mind, i.e. critical 'being'. For example, decisions would not just be retrospectively appraised according to a tick-box set of criteria in order to be justified; rather the process of decision-making would be undertaken with the implicit aim of identifying relevant but alternative decisions right at the start. Similarly, problem-solving would start with questioning the problem itself and gaining different viewpoints on it.

Fook et al. (2000) take this idea further. They show that practice at an expert level is not just about more knowledge and understanding from experience, but about dimensions such as creativity, artistry, openness to new ideas, and also about framing situations in complex rather than routine ways. These dimensions are associated with a process approach to practice that is committed to engaging in a particular way, rather than committed to particular or expected outcomes. A true 'expert' thus approaches any situation as a potentially unpredictable and changeable one by naturally identifying its multifaceted aspects and considering a range of options to 'name and frame' it.

The naming and framing of situations, seen earlier as the essential underlying feature of sound practical reasoning, is one major area where more critical thinking can be triggered automatically, usually by recognition of something not 'normal' – possibly an unexpected action or outcome, or an intuitive feeling of unease. This is where a critical practitioner acknowledges the difference to a usual pattern rather than ignores it, pretends it is OK or standardises it. It is where the benefits of keeping up to date in a professional area of practice and having the necessary critical resources come to the fore. Such a practitioner will have more knowledge and awareness to recognise the incident for what it is, and more self-confidence to deal with it explicitly. The outcomes from such creative and innovative practice can result in transformative development of expertise. An additional area to consider here is the notion of resilience in your own professional field and its links to emotional intelligence (Goleman, 1996).

Development of professional expertise is, therefore, not necessarily dependent on length of experience but rather on a particular disposition and mindset, and the ability to learn from experience. Also, in this respect, we could say that such 'expertise' cannot be defined in prescriptive, narrow terms.

Analytical, and intuitive or instinctive ways of thinking

If we are aiming to embed criticality into the heart of practice we need to be able to understand how our thinking processes work in more detail. Recent research and ideas from Klein's (2004) work on intuition and pattern recognition, and even Kahneman's (2011) work on fast and slow thinking, can be useful here. In the space available we can only touch on these ideas but, in essence, there appear to be two interrelated dimensions of our thinking – slow/analytical (step-by-step, objective and logically defensible process, involving conscious mental effort and self-control) and fast/intuitive (instinctive cognitive responses, effortless and automatic).

The prevailing positivist model of the Western world values rationality and logical, systematic deliberation, and so analytical thinking is traditionally viewed as a superior form of thinking (Dunne, 2011). It is dependent on a belief that we can 'quantify' and control reality and be able to get 'outside' ourselves in order to view a truth or a single right answer that is 'out there' to be found. Of course, any logical, systematic process can help clarify thinking, encourage focus and encourage openness and scrutiny in order to provide accountability. Intuitive thinking, by contrast, can be seen as subjective and therefore unreliable, biased, fallible and untrustworthy. Intuitive thinking can allow a very fast response; it is an active and realistic model; and it can allow accuracy in uncertain situations too (Gigerenzer, 2007). Of course, intuitive thinking is automatic and, therefore, inherently biased to believe and confirm, and then jump to conclusions. However, analytical thinking is not without its faults. It can leave a decision-maker unable to react quickly and effectively, and it can usually only focus on choice at one point in time. The decision-maker can become overwhelmed by the complexity of a task resulting in 'analysis paralysis', and it can also encourage misplaced confidence in an ability to make predictions.

REFLECTION POINT

Is there a 'culture' in your organisation or team that says analytical thinking is more reliable? If so, how does it affect the justification of your more intuitive based decisions?

Of course, our thought processes are more complex than simply being analytical or intuitive. Early research by Isenberg (1984) shows how practising managers depend on a mix of intuition and disciplined analysis, and that intuition is used in all stages of the problem-solving process. When faced with very complex problems managers were seen to usually bypass more analytical and rigorous systematic planning, although they usually justified it later as such. Hammond's (1996) work on a 'cognitive continuum theory of judgement' presents these two dimensions as a continuum and links them to the processing of ill-structured or well-structured judgement tasks, showing that the ill-structured end of the dimension is more likely to engender an intuitive thinking response and vice versa. Kahneman (2011) talks about the uneasy interaction of fast and slow thinking, and argues that even if we think we are using slow analytical thinking to make choices and decisions, we are influenced all the time by our fast intuitive thinking.

For the purposes of this text we would say that Klein's (1998, 2004) work developing a naturalistic model of decision-making (Recognition Primed Decision Making) can prove useful to help us analyse our more intuitive thinking. It provides an interesting set of ideas that help explain how we 'naturally' decide what to do in a fast-moving situation. The two key components are:

1. Sizing up the situation – this involves recognising relevant 'cues' which let you recognise a certain 'pattern'. This relates to the naming and framing idea seen earlier. Once we recognise a pattern we gain a 'sense' of that situation – we know what cues are going to be important and need to be monitored. We know what goals we might be able to accomplish. We have an idea of what to expect next.

2. These patterns also include ideas for a response – a course of action to follow. Identifying a course of action that makes sense for that situation, and then evaluating that course of action by imagining it is the second component.

In other words, recognition of the familiar and non-familiar in a situation means being able to identify cues and their significance – this is pattern matching, which is the first phase. Knowledge of a range of acceptable courses of action and being able to think them through requires mental simulation – this is the second phase. This second phase is also called a singular evaluation approach because each option for action is evaluated in turn and on its own merits in response to the initial pattern matching. (This is in contrast to an analytical model that would initially create a range of differing options in order to evaluate them against each other.)

Large sets of internalised cues and patterns are required in order to size up situations as well as a store of mental models of action to then imagine and evaluate a responsive course of action effectively. So, this approach is reliant on continuing experiential learning to build and update such expertise so that cues and patterns are not only identified but their significance and relevance to the decision is understood too.

ACTIVITY 7.1

Make a brief list of types of work-based learning and support opportunities that could help to develop the type of expertise necessary for both pattern matching and mental simulation, i.e. evaluated and internalised sets of cues, patterns and courses of action. Note in detail how and why your suggested opportunities would achieve this.

Klein (2004) argues that we need to have a greater understanding of the actual dilemmas and decisions underlying the development of expertise – what makes them difficult and what insights might allow us to make those decisions better. So he advocates that any active experiential learning activities (real or simulated) need to explicitly define the decision requirements of the task in order to recognise cues and patterns and build mental models. His decision requirements table includes the following:

- *Identify a critical, difficult and frequent decision or judgement and ask:*

    o *What makes this difficult?*

    o *What kinds of errors are often made?*

    o *How would an expert make this decision differently from a novice? Identify cues and strategies.*

Evidence-informed practice

There is a large amount of debate concerning evidence-informed or evidence-based practice and its place within health and social work. It is not within the remit of this handbook to explore the arguments further and we have already looked at the critical use of formal knowledge for our purposes in Chapter 4. As students within an academic environment you will be expected to gain an understanding of the current theory, research focus and policy development within your studies, and discuss such issues in your assignments. As professionals we have already seen that new knowledge and ideas enhance and develop practice expertise by providing insights from a historical, psychological, sociological, national, international and patient- or service-user perspective. Your depth of involvement with different types of research material will depend on various issues, for example:

- the emphasis of your work within a medical model (which is highly evidence-based);

- the research culture of your organisation.

To sum up an overall position on this issue, we could say that to apply or base practice on any type of evidence without moral or ethical sensitivity, or a wider assessment of context, individual circumstances, situational requirements or risk assessment of possible implications, would be deemed 'uncritical' practice and is unacceptable.

Review

We do not have to pretend we are in a perfect world and always able to do the right thing. What we need to show and evidence is how we take account of the uncertainty and complexity of our role and how we try to work from a critical stance. Thinking critically must not be about feeling threatened or being made to feel inadequate. It is an holistic, open and positive way of approaching the world, and a natural one.

An awareness and acceptance of uncertainty in the practice of any professional is an important way to lessen stress. There are no perfect solutions out there to find, so we cannot be called on to work perfectly. If we accept the fact that the things we do or decide on are still dependent on something uncertain or on future happenings, and work in a way that takes account of that (i.e. constantly reviewing the things we deal with, decide on or do), then this is really what 'thinking critically' is all about.

As Taylor and White (2006) show, critical practice is not about 'being certain' (the 'certain' thing is not necessarily the 'right' thing); it is about being able to deal with uncertainty using sound, valid and accountable processes and, where appropriate, maintaining a position of 'respectful uncertainty', or at least holding on to doubt for longer and seeking out other possible versions. In addition, developing expertise can become a critically constructive practice as well.

How this stance can be used and developed within continuing learning, and facilitated and enabled in others, is the subject of the final chapter.

FURTHER READING

Bradbury, H, Frost, N, Kilminster, S and Zukas, M (eds) (2010) *Beyond reflective practice: New approaches to professional lifelong learning.* London: Routledge.

A look at the new forms of reflective practice that are emerging in different professions which deal with issues such as context and power.

Klein, G (2004) *The power of intuition.* New York: Currency Books.

This book explores intuition as a tangible skill that allows us to recognise patterns and cues as a natural learning process from experience over time.

Chapter 8

Continuing learning: a critical approach

We have explored where criticality fits within established ways of working to foster more critical practice. Now we can look at how it can be developed for ourselves and enabled for others within continuing learning experiences.

CPD, or ongoing work-based learning, can occur in many different ways (from taking part in planned, formal courses through to informal and unplanned day-to-day encounters, or engaging in leadership, research and professional debate activities). Many health and social work practitioners take on team leadership roles or engage in project work to enhance their careers.

We will look first at maximising our own learning from all work-based learning situations as a critically reflective practitioner; second at enabling criticality for other learners; and finally at social learning cultures. Some of these ideas have been drawn from and are explored further in our book *The practice educator's handbook* (Williams and Rutter, 2015).

Maximising ongoing learning

The type of ongoing learning required to develop skills, abilities and attributes in the workplace is multi-layered. There is no single theory of learning in the workplace and, in fact, Cheetham and Chivers (2001) point out the dangers of placing too much reliance on a single approach and argue for seeking to provide exposure to as wide a variety of learning mechanisms as possible. They encourage practitioners to view all experiences as potential learning experiences. In particular, they advocate a mindset of continuing learning from the outset in practice and collaboration with others in learning.

In this respect, practitioners who already have the skills, abilities and attributes of self-directed learners should be able to make the most of the learning potential found within work situations. Those who are lucky enough to work in a positive learning culture that encourages sharing of knowledge, plus feedback and evaluation of services, should be able to truly maximise this potential for themselves and others.

The skills of self-directed (also referred to as autonomous or independent) learning allow practitioners to:

- take the initiative in diagnosing their learning needs;
- create their own learning objectives;
- identify, locate and evaluate the resources needed;
- choose and implement appropriate learning strategies;
- evaluate learning outcomes.

These are useful skills, but, as with any process, a more holistic and critical stance can foster a deeper and more meaningful engagement. For example, here it could encourage a practitioner to actively seek and reflect on more critical feedback from service users or colleagues and gain another perspective.

Also, recognising the need to make the most of informal as well as more formal learning to develop practice becomes a critical habit of mind. Informal learning covers events like observation, feedback, dialogue and co-working, and usually results in new knowing or understanding that is either tacit or regarded as part of a person's general capability, rather than as something 'learnt'. However, it is a key area for professional development. For example, Becher (1999) reports that professionals learn six times as much through non-formal as through formal means.

To make any learning more explicit and meaningful requires a commitment to recording it, reflecting on it, actively using the ideas, etc., in practice and evaluating the outcomes. We can particularly see how critical reflection models (see Chapter 5) could help to lift subconscious or informal learning to a more conscious and formalised level, using critically analytical (how? and why?) and evaluative (how well?) stages. Only such conscious learning and development becomes educative in a true sense (i.e. deep, meaningful and owned), and thus able to impact on the development of professional judgement and expertise, and in turn to enhance service quality.

Enabling others

Professional development is obviously a complex form of growth that is more than the sum of its individual parts and is never complete. A key point is that, as professionals, we will not automatically continue to learn and develop simply because we have gained more experience, or have reflected on it. As mentioned above, increasing experience may have a detrimental effect on learning as the associated increase in confidence can at times lead us into uncritical routine, where we make assumptions and fail to notice the small but possibly crucial differences between one situation and another.

Therefore, the support and facilitation of professional development and the need for health and social workers to play an effective role in developing others (e.g. as practice educators or mentors) becomes an important issue. As enablers of others in the workplace, you will need to focus on more than just 'teaching' specific practice skills and enable all levels of learners to develop not just competence but also the enhanced capability required for critical practice. This type of enablement means working in partnership with individuals and explicitly encouraging them to take responsibility for their practice (Taylor and White, 2006; Williams and Rutter, 2015). This involves so much more than showing or telling someone what to do, providing answers or offering solutions, which can all create dependency. It is about enabling individuals to explore and find answers themselves. This should create flexibility and responsiveness. It is about encouraging, facilitating and supporting learners to critically reflect on and explore their own practice (the deliberation as well as the resulting action), gain confidence in their judgement and expertise, and understand how to develop it further. Of course, these ideas relate to our discussions on developing critical reflection in Chapter 5.

ACTIVITY *8.1*

Review some methods which you, as a qualified practitioner, might use to adopt such a critical questioning stance in order to take account of an individual learner's approach and attitude to their practice, and encourage them to take responsibility for developing that practice.

What differences would there be in your approach and methods between working with a qualifying student and an experienced member of staff?

COMMENT

As we noted earlier, questions and/or learning activities should encourage and support people to think through and develop their own ideas, plus identify and explore the significance of issues and/or experiences. The idea is to enable them to practise working things out for themselves. Understanding what the best methods will be to achieve this can only come from getting to know them first and then working to their strengths in partnership with them. An experienced practitioner's knowledge could provide useful starting points or illustrations, and the approach taken could be as peers working together to resolve certain issues.

Appropriate methods

Open dialogue is a key element in such facilitation, and discussion can happen in many work-based scenarios, e.g. one-to-one, supervision, mentoring, workshops. Remember, there are no 'right' questions to ask learners because there are no clear-cut answers – 'certain' reasons and justifications are not always appropriate when talking about professional knowledge. In fact, it is also about listening correctly, i.e. actively, without interruption or judgement, and about reflecting back what you think you've heard for clarification. Abbott and Taylor (2013) recommend the use of questions in action learning that help colleagues gain new insights by actively enquiring into the other person's views and reasoning, and supporting them to question themselves, especially on aspects they may not have considered previously. They use thinking questions (asking about what is known or understood in order to get a detailed picture and explore facts etc.), feeling questions (asking about what is felt in order to support and challenge this) and willing questions (asking about the drive and motivation to get things done in order to look ahead and take action).

Questioning someone to elicit self-scrutiny of such issues must obviously not become, or be seen as, behaviour that insults, threatens or attacks their self-esteem. It is not what you do, but how the learner perceives that action which will lead to their response. If the learner perceives questioning as threatening in any way (whether you think it is or not), he or she may retreat or attack, and the learning experience will become a very negative situation. Critical questioning therefore involves very skilful framing of insightful and empathetic questions to encourage analysis and challenge thinking. This is a skill that may need training and subsequent refinement (e.g. in coaching) for qualified practitioners enabling others, but many skills may be transferred from the type of work undertaken already with service users. Brookfield (1987, pp93–4) suggests the following general guidelines:

- be specific – relate questions to particular events, situations, people and actions;

- work from the particular to the general – exploring a general theme within the context of a specific event helps people feel they are in familiar territory;

- be conversational – informal, non-threatening tones help people feel comfortable.

We would add another suggestion – be emotionally intelligent (i.e. aware of the effect your questioning is having and watch for any negative signs, e.g. non-response, a defensive position being argued too aggressively, brooding resignation).

Enabling critical refection and practice

Facilitating the critical reflection of others is obviously a difficult balance between providing a safe but appropriately challenging learning situation. As the aim of critical reflection is to create at least some doubt and critique of ongoing actions, the whole process can be extremely anxiety-provoking, especially if a learner is unsure and lacks confidence in the first place. There is another issue to consider as well which relates to criticality. Although many competency-type skills may be easily reflected on and self-appraised, a person's disposition at work and the approaches they take to work situations will be so closely tied in with their personality and previous history that for many a truly honest examination is very difficult to achieve. The requirement for critically and honestly appraising one's own assumptions, deliberations, decisions or actions requires a particular humility alongside a confident allowance of uncertainty. Obviously this is a very complex notion, especially in the early stages of a career when workers are setting out to prove themselves. The need for such honesty and humility especially holds true for the qualified practitioner if they are truly working in a partnership of trust with a learner, i.e. they have to model this behaviour in order to be credible.

If you have successfully enabled someone to critically reflect, then ensuring that there are effective learning outputs from the process is the next step. Help them to scaffold and integrate the knowledge and understanding that results from critical reflection and place it into a work-based context for future use, i.e. covering knowledge, skills and values (knowing, acting and being) for practice itself. This could involve further questioning or designed learning activities, such as the use of other critical incidents, imagined scenarios or role-play.

ACTIVITY 8.2

It can be rather oppressive to insist on learners following specific and prescriptive instructions to 'make' them reflect.

Research some of the models of facilitating reflection seen in Chapter 5 and/or any others that interest you and develop your own model incorporating the features you think are most important. How can you encourage a learner to develop their own 'model' or set of key steps or aspects specific to their needs?

COMMENT

A model should ensure safety as well as challenge for a learner and allow the process to be strengths-based. Most models will aim towards a form of critical analysis which can generate new understanding for future practice, i.e. something meaningful. Understanding and using their particular learning style/s and preferences should help learners create something suited to their particular approaches and ways of working.

To take a wider view on enabling the critical practice of others, we can return to Taylor and White's (2006) idea that critical practice is about being able to deal with uncertainty using sound, valid and accountable processes and, where appropriate, maintaining a position of 'respectful uncertainty'. Gray and Gibbons (2007, p235) advocate that good prudent judgement is an individual virtue that must be cultivated beyond the use of structured, linear decision-making frameworks which tend to develop *the false assumption that the procedures or codes or framework will resolve the ethical problem when, clearly, there are no answers, only choices, and often the right choices make waves.*

Here, a qualified practitioner can help any learner to at least hold on to doubt for longer and seek out other possible versions as suggested. However, being adaptable enough to 'act' in a flexible manner in a wide range of circumstances is a difficult call and there may be many other methods which help foster a more open approach. What may be needed is the opportunity (with appropriate space and freedom, i.e. no risk) to explore alternative approaches and choices wherever possible. This may help reinforce understanding that there is usually more than one possible interpretation or approach to a complex situation, and that there is often no one 'right answer' or 'right way' to do something in professional practice.

Enabling others to practise more critically and reflectively exposes us all to different ways of representing what we do. So the best type of work-based learning can help all participants to see their processes of reasoning and judgement more realistically and to become more *reflexive, analytic and systematic in their sense-making activities* (Taylor and White, 2006, p950). In other words, we may all learn from this involvement in learning; as the relative importance of learning from experience becomes greater, the more expert we become. Perhaps this is a way to build true communities of practice and cultures of learning which reject the separation of training and learning from practice (Lave and Wenger, 1991) and enable the organisation to learn as well. We will briefly look at this as our next area of focus.

Social learning cultures

There is a growing recognition of the central importance of organisations having a culture that supports continuous learning and enables the conversion of individual learning to organisational change.

We have already mentioned that the system we work in, and the people we work with, can affect our opportunities and ability to learn. Here we can look at social and environmental factors for learning effectively. Knight et al. (2006) advocate spaces for the creation of shared meaning, e.g. for collegiality and participation; and for processes such as reflection to capture, codify but also share implicit knowledge. The authors describe professional development as the development of capabilities that actually occur as a consequence of situated social practices and the work-based learning environment.

The idea of ongoing and more critical learning therefore needs to be an embedded part of being a professional and this means that leaders playing their full role in developing appropriate cultures and opportunities for it. Nixon and Murr (2006, p802) take the social/group learning issue further into an analysis of the role of the organisation and show that the organisational context is itself critical to the development of practice learning. They highlight how informal learning is tied up with communities of practice that can supply the social learning opportunities, and argue that practice learning makes a contribution to the quality of professional practice and the organisation's services too. Learning, therefore, does not just remain with the individual; it needs to be appropriately led and transferred in order to create the changes necessary in the organisation for improved performance.

National initiatives promoting a culture of learning are not always enough in themselves to bring about a wide-scale development of learning organisations, but they could help support the development of appropriate 'micro' learning cultures, in which all staff recognise and value the role that they have to play in leading and supporting individual and organisational learning.

This is obviously a huge area for debate and may be an issue you want to discuss or explore further within your programme and/or workplace.

REFLECTION POINT

How can you deal with a negative workplace learning culture?

Which areas of professionalism are likely to suffer?

List any ideas that may enable you to informally lead more collaborative learning in your workplace.

Practical ideas for developing a learning culture include:

- *learning sets, e.g. for post-qualifying study;*
- *mentoring/coaching/induction schemes;*
- *engaging with projects, action research;*
- *staff development to encourage reflective as well as managerial supervision.*

Review

We have tried within this chapter to develop an understanding of how critical practice and the notion of capability can be developed for ourselves and enabled for others within continuing learning experiences. As work-based learners we all need directed but risk-free opportunities to critically analyse and evaluate our practice, and explore alternative approaches wherever possible, in order to deal effectively with the continuing complexity of practice.

FURTHER READING

Beverley, A and Worsley, A (2007) *Learning and teaching in social work practice.* London: Palgrave Macmillan.

A very readable guide to learning and teaching in social work, covering the necessary learning theory as well as the key aspects of the learning partnership.

Gould, N and Baldwin, M (eds) (2004) *Social work, critical reflection and the learning organisation.* Aldershot: Ashgate.

An interesting book that explores the importance of critical reflection in social work and the links between critical reflection and the creation of learning organisations.

Williams, S and Rutter, L (2015) *The practice educator's handbook.* 3rd edition. London: Sage/ Learning Matters.

This book aims to help practitioners develop their own, and others', critical practice in line with the Practice Educator Standards.

Conclusion

As we have seen, our original set of intellectual resources for critical thinking can be applied to all areas of qualifying, post-qualifying and CPD learning, and be aligned with activities such as professional reasoning and judgement, using knowledge in practice, critical reflection, writing and enabling self and others to develop critical practice. It comes down to three basic abilities: questioning, analysing and evaluating, which dovetail into the various methods associated with professional practice development and learning.

Critical reflection can enable the identification, exploration and understanding of practice activities, e.g. practical reasoning, decision-making, managing risk, exercising power and responsibility, using discretion, integrating values. Reflective learning will enable these activities to develop with new knowledge and new experiences. Writing critically allows an appropriate academic structuring and evidencing of this reflection for formal learning, and enables a more thorough critical analysis and evaluation of the knowledge and learning taking place.

This whole process can also constructively move our practice forward to incorporate any necessary change and development. In this way, new knowledge and understanding are developed further for ourselves, for others and for our professions as we begin to develop, articulate and evaluate our expertise. More holistically it develops a way of being as a professional practitioner.

We may not have a lot of time for critical thinking, reflection or writing, and, as abilities or qualities they are processes that need experience and practice in order to be undertaken effectively. CPD learning provides the opportunities for the experience and practice, and can also give you the professional and/or academic credit for doing it. The other good news is that you can develop your abilities by understanding the various elements involved, and by having some methods to follow, adapt and make your own. In this respect we hope this handbook has given you a better understanding, as well as some useful ideas, to work with.

Finally, good judgement, reflecting and writing skills help you to deliver responsive, quality services and be accountable for them. We hope that throughout all your efforts in developing 'critical thinking' the people you serve and work with will benefit.

Appendix 1

Professional Capabilities Framework

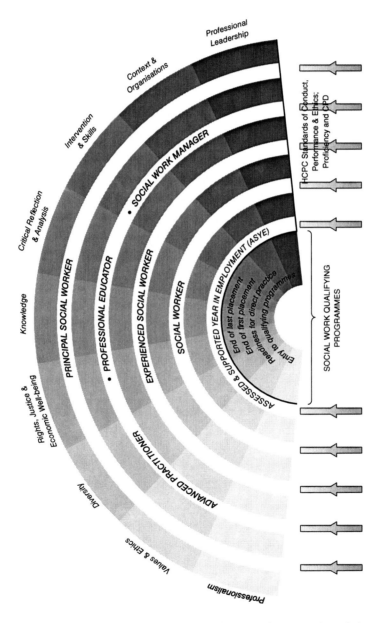

Professional Capabilities Framework diagram reproduced with permission of The College of Social Work

References

Abbott, C and Taylor, P (2013) *Action learning in social work.* London: Sage/Learning Matters.

Adams, R, Dominelli, L and Payne, M (eds) (2009) *Critical practice in social work.* 2nd edition. Basingstoke: Palgrave.

Argyris, C and Schön, D (1974) *Theory in practice: Increasing professional effectiveness.* San Francisco: Jossey Bass.

Atkins, S and Murphy, K (1994) Reflective practice. *Nursing Standard,* 8 (39), 49–56.

Bailin, S, Case, R, Coombs, JR and Daniels, LB (1999) Conceptualizing critical thinking. *Journal of Curriculum Studies,* 31, 285–302.

Barnett, R (1997) *Higher education: A critical business.* Buckingham: Society for Research in Higher Education and Open University Press.

Baxter Magolda, M (1992) *Knowing and reasoning in college.* San Franciso: Jossey Bass.

Becher, Y (1999) *Professional practices: Commitment and capability in a changing environment.* New Brunswick, NJ: Transaction.

Beckett, D and Hager, P (2000) Making judgements as the basis for workplace learning: Towards an epistemology of practice. *International Journal of Lifelong Education,* 19(4), 300–11.

Bondi, L, Carr, D, Clark, C and Clegg, C (eds) (2011) *Towards professional wisdom: Practical deliberation in the people professions.* Farnham: Ashgate.

Bowlby, J (1951) *Maternal care and mental health.* Report to the World Health Organisation. New York: Shocken Books.

Bowlby, J (1969) *Attachment and loss: Attachment.* New York: Basic Books.

Bradbury, H, Frost, N, Kilminster, S and Zukas, M (eds) (2010) *Beyond reflective practice: New approaches to professional lifelong learning.* London: Routledge.

Brockbank, A and McGill, I (1998) *Facilitating reflective learning in higher education.* Buckingham: Society for Research into Higher Education and Open University Press.

Brookfield, S (1987) *Developing critical thinkers.* Milton Keynes: Open University Press.

Brookfield, S (2012) *Teaching for critical thinking: Tools and techniques to help students question their assumptions.* San Francisco: Jossey Bass.

Cameron, S (2009) *Final report from the PBPL funded project: Critical engagement in the MBA.* Milton Keynes: The Open University.

Cheetham, G and Chivers, G (2001) How professionals learn in practice: An investigation of informal learning amongst people working in professions. *Journal of European Industrial Training,* 25 (5), 248–92.

Clark, C (2011) Evidence-based practice and professional wisdom. In: L Bondi, D Carr, C Clark and C Clegg (eds) *Towards professional wisdom: Practical deliberation in the people professions.* Farnham: Ashgate, 45–62.

College of Social Work, England (2012) *Professional capabilities framework.* Available from: www.tcsw.org.uk/home

Cottrell, S (2003) *The study skills handbook.* 2nd edition. London: Palgrave Macmillan.

Cottrell, S (2013) *The study skills handbook.* 4th edition. London: Palgrave Macmillan.

Davys, AM and Beddoe, L (2009) The reflective learning model: Supervision of social work students. *Social Work Education,* 28 (8), 919–33.

Department of Education (2014) *Consultation on knowledge and skills for child and family social work: Government response.* Available from: www.gov.uk/government/uploads/system/uploads

Driscoll, JJ (2000) *Practising clinical supervision: A reflective approach.* London: Bailliere Tindall (in association with the RCN).

Dunne, J (2011) *Professional wisdom in practice.* In: L Bondi, D Carr, C Clark and C Clegg (eds) *Towards professional wisdom: Practical deliberation in the people professions.* Farnham: Ashgate, 13–26.

Ellett, FS (2012) Practical rationality and recovery of Aristotle's 'phronesis' for the professions. In: EA Kinsella and A Pitman (eds) *Phronesis as professional knowledge: Practical wisdom in the professions.* Rotterdam: Sense Publishers, 13–34.

Eraut, M (1994) *Developing professional knowledge and competence.* London: Routledge.

Fook, J, Ryan, M and Hawkins, L (2000) *Professional expertise: Practice, theory and education for working in uncertainty.* London: Whiting & Birch.

Ford, P, Johnston, B, Mitchell, R and Myles, F (2004) Social work education and criticality: Some thoughts from research. *Social Work Education,* 23 (2), 185–98.

Ford, P, Johnston, B, Mitchell, R and Myles, F (2005) Practice learning and the development of students as critical practitioners: Some findings from research. *Social Work Education,* 24 (4), 391–407.

Francis, R (2013) Report of the Mid Staffordshire NHS Foundation Trust Public Inquiry. London: The Stationery Office.

Gibbs, G (1998) *Learning by doing: A guide to teaching and learning methods.* Birmingham: SCED.

Gibbs, L and Gambrill, E (1999) *Critical thinking for social workers: Exercises for the helping profession.* London: Sage.

Gibbs, L and Gambrill, E (2002) *Evidence-based practice: Counter arguments to objections. Research on Social Work Practice,* 12 (3), 452–76.

Gigerenzer, G (2007) *Gut feelings: Short cuts to better decision making.* London: Penguin Books.

Goleman, D (1996) *Emotional intelligence.* London: Bloomsbury.

Gray, M and Gibbons, J (2007) There are no answers, only choices: Teaching ethical decision making in social work. *Australian Social Work,* (60) 2, 222–38.

Hamill, C (1999) Academic essay writing in the first person: A guide for undergraduates. *Nursing Standard,* 13 (44), 38–40.

Hammond, KR (1996) *Human judgment and social policy: Irreducible uncertainty, inevitable error, unavoidable injustice.* New York: Oxford University Press.

Hibbert, K (2012) Cultivating capacity: Phronesis, learning, and diversity in professional education. In: EA Kinsella and A Pitman (eds) *Phronesis as professional knowledge: Practical wisdom in the professions.* Rotterdam: Sense Publishers, 61–72.

Isenberg, D (1984) How senior managers think. *Harvard Business Review,* Nov–Dec (84608).

Ixer, G (1999) There's no such thing as reflection. *British Journal of Social Work,* 29, 513–27.

Ixer, G (2010) There's no such thing as reflection: Ten years on. *The Journal of Practice Teaching in Health and Social Work,* 10 (1), 75–93.

Johns, C (1998) Opening the doors of perception. In: C Johns and D Freshwater (eds) *Transforming nursing through reflective practice.* Oxford: Blackwell Science.

Kahneman, D (2011) *Thinking, fast and slow.* London: Penguin Books.

Kandlbinder, P (2007) Writing about practice for future learning. In: D Baud and N Falchikov (eds) *Rethinking assessment in higher education: Learning for the longer term.* New York: Routledge, 159–66.

Kemmis, S (2012) Phronesis, experience and the primacy of praxis. In: EA Kinsella and A Pitman (eds) *Phronesis as professional knowledge: Practical wisdom in the professions.* Rotterdam: Sense Publishers, 147–62.

Kinsella, EA and Pitman, A (eds) (2012) *Phronesis as professional knowledge: Practical wisdom in the professions.* Rotterdam: Sense Publishers.

Klein, G (1998) *Sources of power: How people make decisions.* London: MIT Press.

Klein, G (2004) *The power of intuition.* New York: Currency Books.

Knight, P, Tait, J and Yorke, M (2006) The professional learning of teachers in higher education. *Studies in Higher Education,* 31 (3), 319–39.

Kolb, DA (1984) *Experiential learning: Experience as the source of learning and development.* New Jersey: Prentice Hall.

Kondrat, M (1992) Reclaiming the practical: Formal and substantive rationality in social work practice. *Social Service Review,* 66 (2), 237–55.

Korthagen, F and Vasalos, A (2005) Levels in reflection: Core reflection as a means to enhance professional development. *Teachers and Teaching: Theory and Practice,* 11 (1), 47–71.

Lave, J and Wenger, E (1991) *Situated learning: Legitimate peripheral participation.* Cambridge: Cambridge University Press.

Lester, S (1995) Beyond knowledge and competence: Towards a framework for professional education. *Capability,* 1 (3), 44–52.

Macaulay, C (2000) Transfer of learning. In: VE Cree and C Macaulay (eds) *Transfer of learning in professional and vocational education.* London: Routledge, 1–26.

Macklin, R and Whiteford, G (2012) Phronesis, aporia, and qualitative research. In: EA Kinsella and A Pitman (eds) *Phronesis as professional knowledge: Practical wisdom in the professions.* Rotterdam: Sense Publishers, 87–100.

Marton, F and Saljo, R (1976) On qualitative differences in learning: 1. Outcome and process. *British Journal of Educational Psychology,* 46, 4–11.

Mathews, I and Crawford, K (2011) *Evidence-based practice in social work.* Exeter: Learning Matters.

Mezirow, J (1981) A critical theory of adult learning and education. *Adult Education,* 32 (1), 3–24.

Moon, J (1999a) *Learning journals: A handbook for academics, students and professional development.* London: Kogan Page.

Moon, J (1999b) *Reflection in learning and professional development: Theory and practice.* London: Kogan Page.

Munro, E (2011) *The Munro Review of Child Protection: Final report. A child-centred system.* Department for Education. Cm 8062. Norwich: The Stationery Office.

Newell, R (1992) Anxiety, accuracy and reflection: The limits of professional development. *Journal of Advanced Nursing,* 17, 1326–33.

Newman, T (2000) *Developing evidence based practice in social care: Locating, appraising and using research findings on effectiveness. Guidelines for practitioners.* Exeter: CEBSS.

Nixon, S and Murr, A (2006) Practice learning and the development of professional practice. *Social Work Education,* 25 (8), 798–811.

Philips, V and Bond, C (2004) Undergraduates' experiences of critical thinking. *Higher Education Research and Development,* 23 (3), 276–94.

QAAHE (2008) *The framework for higher education qualifications in England, Wales and Northern Ireland.* London: Quality Assurance Agency for Higher Education.

Race, P (2001) *The lecturer's toolkit.* 2nd edition. London: Kogan Page.

Rolfe, G, Freshwater, D and Jasper, M (2011) *Critical reflection in practice: Generating knowledge for care.* 2nd edition. London: Palgrave Macmillan.

Schön, D (1983) *The reflective practitioner: How professionals think in action.* London: Temple Smith.

Schön, D (1987) *Educating the reflective practitioner.* London: Temple Smith.

Sellman, D (2012) Reclaiming competence for professional phronesis. In EA Kinsella and A Pitman (eds) *Phronesis as professional knowledge: Practical wisdom in the professions.* Rotterdam: Sense Publishers, 115–30.

Smith, F (1992) *To think: In language, learning and education.* London: Routledge.

Sotto, E (1994) *When teaching becomes learning: A theory and practice of teaching.* London: Continuum.

Standing, M (2010) *Clinical judgement and decision making in nursing and interprofessional healthcare.* Maidenhead: Open University Press/McGraw Hill.

Streumer, B (2009) Practical reasoning. In: T O'Connor and C Sandis (eds) *The Blackwell companion to the philosophy of action.* Oxford: Blackwell.

Taylor, B (2013) *Professional decision making and risk in social work.* 2nd edition. London: Sage/Learning Matters.

Taylor, CP and White, S (2006) Knowledge, truth and reflexivity: The problem of judgement in social work. *Journal of Social Work,* 1 (37), 37–59.

Thompson, N (2006) *Promoting workplace learning.* Bristol: Policy Press.

Thompson, S and Thompson, N (2008) *The critically reflective practitioner.* London: Palgrave Macmillan.

Van Manen, M (1995) On the epistemology of reflective practice. *Teachers and Teaching: Theory and Practice,* 1 (1), 33–50.

Weick, A, Rapp, C, Sullivan, WP and Kristhardt, W (1989) A strengths perspective for social work practice. *Social Work,* 34, 350–4.

Wilkins, D and Boahen, G (2013) *Critical analysis skills for social workers.* Maidenhead: Open University Press/McGraw Hill.

Williams, S and Rutter, L (2015) *The practice educator's handbook.* 3rd edition. London: Sage/Learning Matters.

Index

CPSIA information can be obtained at www.ICGtesting.com
Printed in the USA
LVOW09s0356011215

464710LV00024BA/1325/P